The Theætetus of Plato

Plato, Paley, F. A. (Frederick Apthorp)

BIBLIOLIFE

THE

THEÆTETUS OF PLATO

TRANSLATED, WITH INTRODUCTION AND BRIEF
EXPLANATORY NOTES,

BY

F. A. PALEY, M.A.,

TRANSLATOR OF THE "PHILEBUS," ETC., AND PROFESSOR OF CLASSICAL
LITERATURE IN THE CATHOLIC UNIVERSITY COLLEGE, KENSINGTON.

LONDON:

GEORGE BELL & SONS, YORK STREET, COVENT GARDEN
CAMBRIDGE: DEIGHTON, BELL, AND CO.
1875

INTRODUCTION.

THE subject of the *Theætetus* is the inquiry, *What is Knowledge?* This question might be put, and perhaps in a form more familiar to ourselves, *What is Truth?* Everyone who has thought at all knows how difficult is the answer. The thinkers of old,[1] bewildered by the differences of opinion that prevailed on all speculative subjects, concluded that nothing was certainly true that did not fall under the cognizance of the senses. Thus: 'I am *quite certain* that fire is hot, or that this stone is hard, *because* I feel it so. But I am *not* sure that God exists, or that this action is right or wrong, because moral and metaphysical questions do not fall within the province of *sense*. They are only matters of conviction, and people do not agree about them.'

The existence then of any positive or objective truth residing outside of things phenomenal and independent of opinion, was denied by this school. Plato is constantly cavilling at it; these are 'the giants who can only clutch at sticks and stones'[2]; 'those who think nothing *is* but what

---

[1] "All the old philosophers identified, or at any rate did not distinguish, thinking and sensation or feeling; καὶ οἴ γε ἀρχαῖοι τὸ φρονεῖν καὶ τὸ αἰσθάνεσθαι ταὐτὸν εἶναί φασιν. And that there may be no doubt as to the meaning of ἀρχαῖοι, Aristotle (*Metaph.* iii. 5 1002. 6 12. seq) specifies Parmenides and Empedocles and Anaxagoras and Democritus as philosophers who fell into this error, that is to say, it was shared by all the Pre-Socratic speculators, including even Democritus, who was a somewhat younger contemporary of Socrates." —(*Mr. Cope, on Mr. Grote's Criticisms of the Theætetus*, p. 20)

[2] *Sophist.* p 246. A, *ibid* 247 C, διατείνοιντ' ἂν πᾶν, ὃ μὴ δυνατοὶ ταῖς χερσὶ ξυμπιέζειν εἰσὶν, ὡς ἄρα τοῦτο οὐδὲν τὸ παράπαν ἐστίν.

they can grasp with their hands, and do not accept in the
category of Being the operations of nature in the worlds
beyond our human ken.'[1] This was the state of a soul that
had too long been the servant of the body, μηδὲν ἄλλο δοκεῖν
εἶναι ἀληθὲς ἀλλ᾽ ἢ τὸ σωματοειδές, οὗ τις ἂν χρήσαιτο καὶ
ἴδοι καὶ πίοι καὶ φάγοι καὶ πρὸς τὰ ἀφροδίσια χρήσαιτο.[2]
The Epicureans, with their tendency to materialism, and
apparently following Democritus, seem especially to have
insisted on the tangible only being *knowable* (γνωστόν).
Lucretius strongly affirms this, (i. 422):

> Corpus enim per se communis dedicat esse
> Sensus; cui nisi prima fides fundata valebit
> Haud erit occultis de rebus quo referentes
> Confirmare animi quicquam ratione queamus.

Again, (i. 699):

> Quid nobis certius ipsis
> Sensibus esse potest, qui vera ac falsa notemus?

And elsewhere he says *touch* is the only true test of corporeal
existence, (ii. 434)

> Tactus enim, tactus, pro divum numina sancta,
> Corporis est sensus,

where the apostrophe to the gods shows that he is enunciat-
ing and insisting on what he considers a solemn truth.

Now it was to combat this view, so generally held by his
predecessors and contemporaries, and apparently even by
Protagoras, that Plato composed the *Theætetus.* He shows
by many subtle arguments that *perception* (αἴσθησις), so far
from being the sole test of truth, is in many cases untrust-
worthy, and that for this and other reasons it cannot be the
same as, or even the basis of, exact knowledge (ἐπιστήμη).

---

[1] *Theæt.* p. 155. E.
[2] *Phædo.* p. 81. B.

The general untrustworthiness of external impressions had been strongly insisted on in the *Phaedo* (p. 83. A).[1] Plato's favourite doctrine of abstract truth, as something far higher and more real than mere appearances, and his celebrated theory of the ἰδέαι, or eternal, unchangeable, universal, and typically perfect existences,[2] induced him specially to insist on the necessity of a psychological theory of the mode of apprehension, as opposed to the empirical or merely sensuous kind of knowledge, which varied with fashion, country, age, state of health, and with every change of condition and every caprice of the human mind. It seems probable that this doctrine of abstract (as contrasted with concrete and phenomenal) existence had met with considerable opposition in rival schools; and this supposition will explain the remarkable animosity which Plato shows to a certain school, represented perhaps by Antisthenes, whose disciples he has been thought to describe[3] as σκληροὶ καὶ ἀντίτυποι ἄνθρωποι, —men who defined Being and Body to be identical, and, if anyone asserted the existence of anything not possessed of a body, held him in contempt and refused to hear from him any such doctrine[4] It will explain also the well-known passage in Aristotle,[5] where he apologizes for preferring

---

[1] ἡ φιλοσοφία—ἐνδεικνυμένη ὅτι ἀπάτης μὲν μεστὴ ἡ διὰ τῶν ὀμμάτων ὄψις, ἀπάτης δὲ ἡ διὰ τῶν ὤτων καὶ τῶν ἄλλων αἰσθήσεων, πείθουσα δὲ ἐκ τούτων μὲν ἀναχωρεῖν ὅσον μὴ ἀνάγκη αὐτοῖς χρῆσθαι, αὐτὴν δὲ εἰς αὐτὴν ξυλλέγεσθαι καὶ ἀθροίζεσθαι παρακελευομένη, πιστεύειν δὲ μηδενὶ ἄλλῳ ἀλλ' ἢ αὐτὴν αὑτῇ, ὅτι ἂν νοήσῃ αὐτὴ καθ' αὑτὴν αὐτὸ καθ' αὑτὸ τῶν ὄντων.

[2] *Phaedo* p. 74. A, σκόπει δή, ἦ δ' ὃς, εἰ ταῦτα οὕτως ἔχει· φαμέν πού τι εἶναι ἴσον, οὐ ξύλον λέγω ξύλῳ οὐδὲ λίθον λίθῳ οὐδ' ἄλλο τῶν τοιούτων οὐδέν, ἀλλὰ παρὰ ταῦτα πάντα ἕτερόν τι, αὐτὸ τὸ ἴσον —*Ibid.* p 76—7. See *Respubl.* p. 596.   [3] *Theæt.* p. 156. A

[4] *Sophist* p 246 B. Mr. Campbell however (Introduction to the *Theætetus,* p xxx) thinks that certain atomists, followers of Democritus, may be meant.

[5] *Eth. N.* 1. 4.

truth to the theories of a friend, and holds himself bound to show the fallacy, or, at least, the wholly unpractical nature, of Plato's doctrine of εἴδη, or abstract existences. He asks how can abstract man, for instance, be conceived to differ from actual or particular man, αὐτοάνθρωπος from ἄνθρωπος, since the definition and description of both must be the same.

Plato then (it seems reasonable to suppose) set himself to the task of combating these objectors to his doctrine of abstracts, and undertook to show that sensuous perception is altogether deceptive and worthless as a test of truth. With some satire, we may surmise, on those who professed to teach knowledge while they were unable to define what knowledge was, the real object (or at least, the scope) of the *Theætetus* extends far deeper and wider, and embraces the whole question whether there is such a thing as positive or objective truth at all. Protagoras had either categorically or by implication denied this, by asserting that every man is his own sole test of truth, μέτρον ἕκαστος. And this he had not limited to mere matters of bodily feeling, as heat or cold, sour or sweet, but had extended to moral questions, and affirmed that an act became just or unjust according as the law had sanctioned or forbidden it, and that there was no natural right or wrong in human actions at all.[1] And indeed, it seems impossible to lay down the exact line where the μέτρον ἕκαστος ceases to be a test; for if it is true for determining hot or cold to each person, *i. e.* to his bodily feelings, it may be true *to him*, *i. e.* to his conscience, or

---

[1] *Theæt.* p. 167. C, οἷα ἂν ἑκάστῃ πόλει δίκαια καὶ καλὰ δοκῇ, ταῦτα καὶ εἶναι αὐτῇ, ἕως ἂν αὐτὰ νομίζῃ Hence the νομικὸν and φυσικὸν δίκαιον discussed by Aristotle, *Eth. N. V.* 10, as branches of πολιτικὸν δίκαιον.

mental feeling, as a test of right and wrong Nor is it very
easy to combat the position, that practices are right *because*
the law sanctions them, and wrong *because* it forbids them,
when we entertain the question of the abstract right or
wrong of revenge, polygamy, slavery, or the tenure of property, which inherently and naturally belongs to the strong,
though the law steps in and secures it conventionally for the
weak [1] If every man is his own test of truth, he needs the
opinion of no one; and thus results the apparent paradox,
that every man is as wise as every other man.[2] Protagoras
evaded a conclusion which would have been fatal to his own
claims to superior wisdom as a teacher, by saying[3] that
wisdom consisted in causing others to hold better views by
making the men themselves better, and that men who could
do this were really wiser, though the views they taught were
not, strictly speaking, *truer*, because that only *is* true to
each which he thinks and believes to be true.

"The general question involved in the discussion of the
Protagorean dictum, is of the most real and serious importance : it is no mere dialectical encounter of wits between
Plato and Protagoras, but is of the highest and universal
interest. The question in fact amounts to this : is there
any such thing as truth ? If so, what is it ? Is there any
standard of truth and knowledge independent of ourselves,
our own feelings and momentary consciousness ? Or are we
doomed to be for ever the sport of our own individual fancies
and subjective impressions ?"[4]

According to the doctrine of Protagoras, then, all forms of
religious belief, depending as they do on individual con-

---

[1] *Gorgias*, p 483. B.   [2] *Theæt.* p 161 D.
[3] *Theæt.* p 166. D.   [4] Mr. Cope, *ut sup* p. 8.

viction, are alike true to those who hold them. For as
all alike appeal to *some* external evidence or authority
alleged to be supernatural, each in this respect is precisely
in the same position as the rest. Protagoras would have
denied that any one form of belief had an absolute inherent
truth, because no other standard could be obtained to prove
it to be true; or, by consequence, that the others were false.
Yet in fact, men do both act and argue as if some particular
form of belief must be *ipso facto* and absolutely true, because
they firmly believe it themselves It never occurs to them
to allow that they cannot possibly go further than the allega-
tion that it is true *to them.* There is nothing objective that
they can appeal to, except such evidence or testimony as
(usually without any serious examination) satisfies *them.*
They never listen to or value for a moment the opinion
of others, who may be quite as good and learned as themselves, that they are mistaken in their belief.[1] It is quite
evident then that the issue of this question is of the gravest
possible significance. It intimately affects the whole theory
of right or wrong, and of conscience itself, which at best
is a purely subjective test. If Socrates thought it his duty
to remain in prison and calmly await his execution, then
to him that course was right; while to the friends who
wished to procure his escape,[2] his resolution was wrong,
it was perversely sacrificing a valuable life for a whim and

---

[1] *Theæt* p. 170 D, ὅταν σὺ κρίνας τι παρὰ σαυτῷ πρός με ἀποφαίνῃ περί
τινος δόξαν, σοὶ μὲν δὴ τοῦτο κατὰ τὸν ἐκείνου λόγον ἀληθὲς ἔστω, ἡμῖν δὲ δὴ
τοῖς ἄλλοις περὶ τῆς σῆς κρίσεως πότερον οὐκ ἔστι κριταῖς γενέσθαι, ἢ ἀεί σε
κρίνομεν ἀληθῆ δοξάζειν. It is obvious that, if the world had fully accepted
Protagoras' view, dogmatism and intolerance would have been without a history.
But the human mind is so constituted, that it will not rest without a sense of
assurance; and practically, the assurance that one is right means the assurance
that others (perhaps all others) are wrong.   [2] *Crito*, p. 45. B.

a caprice. Mr. Cope presses this point very strongly: "The truth or falsehood of Protagoras' opinion is in reality a matter of no slight importance to ourselves, quite independently of Plato's success or failure in refuting it; for it seems to involve nothing less than the possibility of[1] the very existence and reality of truth and knowledge. For if each individual man and his own thoughts and feelings, whatever their quality and character and duration, are to be set up as the sole measure and standard of truth and right, it is difficult to conceive how any truth, reality, or knowledge worthy of the name is possible at all."

It is remarkable that Plato, in refuting Protagoras' theory, as set forth in a work which its author had called 'Αλήθεια, shows no certain conviction, and makes no definite statement, of the existence of any objective standard of truth and knowledge whatever. Mr. Cope, however, thinks that, "from occasional hints dropped here and there throughout the course of the dialogue, the author does recognize some objective standard of truth and knowledge, and that the latter must be characterised by universality, constancy, invariability; though this, like the former, is merely suggested, and left to the reader's ingenuity to make out."[2]

It is pretty evident, indeed, that, in writing the *Theætetus*, Plato was feeling his way to some better definition of knowledge, and was reviewing the various modes of apprehension in order to find some test or standard of truth which should be less liable to caprice and error than mere sensation. He was the first to set up a psychological against an æsthetic theory, a course quite in accordance with his

---

[1] (In place of the word *of* (p. 22) there is a comma in Mr. Cope's text, which I think must be a misprint)   [2] p 7.

habitual depreciation of body as not only not favouring, but being adverse to φρόνησις.[1]

There were other modes of stating the same proposition, that "what seems to every man, that is so to him." One was the relativity of knowledge. Nothing exists absolutely, but only in relation to some percipient. Every patient implies an agent, every subject an object, and the converse. No quality or condition *is*, it only *comes into existence* for somebody, and it is therefore only particular, not universal. Οὐδὲν ἔστιν, ἀλλὰ πάντα γίγνεται.[2] Thus, sugar is not sweet, pepper is not pungent, grass is not green in itself, a tongue and an eye must exist to and for which the taste and the colour are brought into being by the act of contact And the statement is perfectly true ; sugar has no natural or inherent sweetness of its own ; it is not sweet in any other sense than *potentially*, viz because the molecules of it affect the nerves or the glands of the palate in one way, as pepper does in another, as Lucretius very truly taught (ii. 420).

On this view therefore knowledge must be special, and wine may taste sour and disagreeable to a disordered palate, while it is pleasant to a healthy one. Nor can you argue with your patient that it is not sour to him. You must cure him, and the pleasant taste will return of itself.[3]

The remarkable discovery of Heraclitus (for so it may be called, since modern science is entirely in accord with it)

---

[1] This was a weak point in all eastern theories of asceticism. To punish the body in order to detach from it, and elevate above it, the soul, was too often to ignore the plain laws of nature, and the good old rule, "mens sana in corpore sano " Though excess stupifies, deficiency of food and bodily comfort will impair the mental faculties. "Phosphates" and "brain-power" are not less real than "mind" and "soul".

[2] p. 152. D.   [3] p. 167 A.

that *motion* is the universal law, and that nothing can ever be really for a moment at rest, πάντα ρεῖ, is a third formula by which individual perception is limited to momentary impression; and therefore, if no impression or effect can be lasting, nothing can be really true to any but the person who at any moment perceives the particular effect. I paint a wall white, which at the end of the year becomes dingy. Every instant of time the dinginess is increasing, the ἀλ-λοίωσις or alteration is a movement that is going on without the least check. Consequently, even when I say that wall "is white," I state what cannot be really true; for during the instant of pronouncing the word, "is" or "white," the change is going on; you cannot assert that it *is* white, since the term "is" fixes the existence of whiteness. The opposite school,[1] who regarded the universe and all within it as fixed and immoveable (the οἱ στασιῶται, as Plato calls them in playful contrast with the οἱ ρέοντες) were the stern opponents of the Ephesian enthusiasts who were followers of Heraclitus,[2] and were perhaps headed by Antisthenes and the Cynics.

All these considerations militate against the idea of *truth*

[1] That of the Eleatics, the followers of Parmenides, whose primary dogma was unity, being, uniformity, and consequently rest.

[2] It is singular that Heraclitus, who taught (though perhaps in a theological as much as in a cosmical or physical sense) that all things were composed of fire, —which seems a near approximation to the modern view of the ultimate identity of heat, force, and motion,—should have been the special object of attack both of Plato and Lucretius (i 638). He rightly saw that motion was the generating as well as the preserving principle of all things. That air and sea have circulating currents as well as plants and animals, he must be considered to have forecast by a wonderful sagacity. So the νοῦς of Anaxagoras, and the subtle principle which, Lucretius teaches (iii 243), forms an ingredient in the *anima*, or vital principle, seems as near an approach to electricity as was possible, short of the actual enunciation of it.

being an absolute or permanent entity; and when we affirm that such a proposition as that $2 \times 2 = 4$ is absolute truth, we can only explain this to mean that all human experience points to the fact, and no diversity of opinion exists about it. It is not so easy to prove, that if a man insists that the world is flat or immoveable, or that the sun goes round the earth, it is not true. It is not true to us, who believe facts are against it; but it is quite as true to him, who believes facts are in favour of it. Here, too, Protagoras would have said, "Don't try to prove his opinion to be wrong. It is *not* wrong to him. Teach him more accurate principles of reasoning, and more careful observation, and the other and better view will become true to him of itself."

The first part of the *Theætetus* is occupied with showing the many ways in which αἴσθησις, or perception, is deceptive. And as ἐπιστήμη means real, constant, unchanging knowledge, it must be something distinct from sensation, which can only be particular. The latter part of the treatise discusses the possibility of knowledge being δόξα, "judgment formed on experience," ὀρθὴ δόξα, "correct estimate," or ὀρθὴ δόξα μετὰ λόγου, that is, when you can give a reason for holding that particular opinion and not another. In the general conclusion, that no man can say what knowledge is or in what faculty it resides, there seems, as we have said, to be some satire on the rival systems which all claimed alike severally to impart knowledge. Whether Plato really thought knowledge, in its absolute sense, unattainable, seems left uncertain. But his constant reference to φρόνησις, the pure intellect to be attained only in an after life, points to this conclusion rather than to any other.[1]

[1] Mr. Campbell observes (Introd. p. lxii.) that "it is not by any means

Mr. Grote's strictures on Plato, that he has misrepresented Protagoras, and that Protagoras did not mean to deny the possibility of knowledge consisting in mental apprehension as well as in mere sense, have been elaborately answered by Mr. Cope in the treatise already referred to. Mr. Cope contends that Plato must have perfectly understood the doctrine of Protagoras, and been fully aware of its logical consequences; and he does not think Plato would have knowingly misrepresented one of whom he always speaks with at least the semblance of respect. "We may therefore conclude" (he says, p 20) "that Protagoras with all his versatility and manifold accomplishments was not in advance of his age in psychological knowledge, and, like his contemporaries, made no distinction between thinking and sensation or feeling."

The series of arguments by which Plato shows αἴσθησις to be deceptive, and in its very nature something distinct from knowledge, is very ingenious and logically conclusive. The first is (p. 152. B), that perception cannot imply real (universal) existence, since it is but the sense of the individual; it may be hot to me but cold to you, and it is impossible to have *knowledge*[1] of anything so capricious, and so purely a matter of fancy. The second is, that as all effects are transient, and brought into being for the particular person who at the moment feels them, they have no οὐσία at all, but only a γένεσις, and therefore cannot be the subject

Plato's intention to point out the hopelessness of the attempt to define knowledge. What he does point out is the impossibility of conceiving Knowledge apart from its object." Apparently, the proposition is a paradox, since everyone talks familiarly of himself or others being "mistaken," *i. e.* every one practically assumes the possibility of error

[1] If a thermometer tells you it *is* hot, it may still feel cold *to you.*

of ἐπιστήμη (p. 153—4). The third, that as all things are
constantly shifting, there can be no *real* αἴσθησις of anything,
even for a moment (p. 156. 7. and 181. C.) The fourth is,
that in morals at least (right and wrong), αἴσθησις can have
no place whatever, and therefore cannot form our knowledge
of them (p. 157. D). The fifth, that in dreams, mad-fits,
delusions, our perceptions are avowedly false (p. 158), and
if we are asleep and dreaming for half our lives, one half of
our sensations must be false. The sixth (p. 159), that the
same thing seems or feels different to us at different times;
and so far from αἴσθησις being ἐπιστήμη, it makes a thing
at once to be the same and something else. The seventh
(p. 160), turns on the *relativity* of knowledge, which of
necessity implies a subject and an object; and the effects
being special to individuals, cannot be universal, and so are
not the subjects of true knowledge. The eighth (p. 163), is
that perception must imply cognition; it falls short in itself
of conveying that apprehension which we mean by knowledge. The ninth (p. 163. D), that a knowledge of something
gained by experience remains in the mind after the actual
αἴσθησις is past, and is quite distinct from it; and therefore
ἐπιστήμη cannot be the same as αἴσθησις. The tenth
(p. 164), that on the hypothesis of αἴσθησις being ἐπιστήμη,
a man can have no knowledge by memory,—he must be
ignorant of what he knows by sight, should he chance to
shut his eyes. The eleventh (p. 165. B), that a man may at
once know and not know the same thing, if he sees it with
one eye but not with the other. The twelfth (p. 165. D),
that we apply terms to the *senses*, which are inapplicable to
mental apprehension; you may 'see an object near', but no
one talks of 'understanding a subject near', etc. The

thirteenth and last (p. 178), that knowledge may be prospective, as a cook knows that a seasoned dish will be
palatable, or an orator knows that a speech will 'take',
whereas αἴσθησις is of *present* effects only. In such cases
there *certainly* is such a thing as superior intelligence;
whence it follows, that not all knowledge is to be brought
to the standard of present feeling or perception.

The general conclusion is arrived at (p. 184. E), that
there must be some mental faculty or mode of apprehension
beyond mere sensuous perception; in other words, that every
perception involves some conception. You cannot see a
horse, for instance, without the mental conceptions of its
colour, size, motion, existence, distinctness from other animals,
etc. Knowledge therefore is a mixed process of experience
and intuition,—of thought consequent on perception.

In the latter part of the *Theœtetus* (from p. 187) Plato
proceeds to examine Opinion (δόξα), as a kind of knowledge
distinct from sense, and as a pure act of the intellect.

" Considered quite in the abstract" (says Mr. Campbell,[1]),
" false opinion seems impossible. For whenever we think,
our thought is known to us, and real. Or, if thinking be
a silent proposition, it seems impossible that we should join
two ideas wrongly when both are clearly present to the
mind."

Opinion is a "judgment formed on sensation,"[2] and the
forming it is a process between thought and perception.
And "false opinion will thus be the failure of the mind in
bringing together the impressions of sensation and memory."[3]

Plato's argument is certainly not very easy to follow,

[1] Introduction to *Theœt*. p. lx   [2] Mr. Cope, p. 6.
[3] Mr Campbell, *ibid.* See *Philebus*, p 39 A

but it turns mainly on the point, that every conception, being of *something*, must be real, *i.e.* must have an *οὐσία*, to him who conceives it. And if it is real, it cannot be false in the sense of non-existent. To mistake one thing for another, if apart from sensation, is at once 'to know and not to know', *i.e.* to know a subject and yet not know its difference from another. If combined with sense (*e.g.* when we see a stranger approach, and mistake him in the distance for a friend, or what we call 'mistaken identity'), it is when the memory is at variance with the impression of the senses. Plato treats exhaustively all the cases where knowledge and sensation, sensation without knowledge, or knowledge without sensation, are concerned; and he concludes[1] that mistaken opinion can only occur when the mind knows and remembers two distinct objects, but, from defective sight or other sense, applies the memory of one to the perception of the other. In a word, apart from *sensation* there is no false opinion properly so-called [2]

The nearest approximation to knowledge would seem to be "right opinion for which one can give a reason" (*μετὰ λόγου*). A man who can give an account of an eclipse, and explain why it occurs, may fairly be said to have a knowledge of it. But here occurs a difficulty · unless one knows the elements or first conditions of things, can one be said to *know* them in their results or combinations? If one does not know what gold and copper are, *i e* how they are formed

---

[1] *περὶ ὧν ἴσμεν τε καὶ αἰσθανόμεθα, ἐν αὐτοῖς τούτοις στρέφεται καὶ ἑλίττεται ἡ δόξα ψευδὴς καὶ ἀληθὴς γιγνομένη, ibid.* " In the sphere between sense and knowledge lies the region of error, in the observations of sense and the judgments pronounced upon them."—*Mr. Cope*, p. 30.

[2] *Theæt.* p 193. B. Thus a short-sighted man says to his friend, ' I mistook you for A or B.'

and what are their constituents, can one be said to *know*
what 'Jeweller's gold' is, compounded of the two, merely
by giving that account of it ? If no account can be given of
separate letters, A, B, C, have we a right to say we *know*
them in combination, CAB ? Or has combination (συλλα-
βὴ) a character or ἰδέα of its own, without regard to its
being made up of parts ? To show this, it is necessary to
show that ὅλον may be different from πάντα μέρη, though it
contains them all, potentially at least. And certainly a
whole loaf is something different in its nature from the
twelve slices into which it has been cut.

Strictly speaking, therefore, the complex does not *consist*
of the elements in combination, though it contains them.
It has an independent form, character, and being, εἶδος and
οὐσία, *i. e.* as the complex distinct from the simple. Hence
the power of analysis does not suffice to constitute knowledge, and the addition of μετὰ λόγου to ὀρθὴ δόξα will not
bring 'right opinion' really nearer to true knowledge

That "more or less," "greater or smaller," are purely
relative, and have no absolute existence, is shown by the
comparison of four dice with six, the sizes of a boy and
man with a post, etc.[1] Such ideas as time, space, size,
distance, number, are only relative, being indeterminate and
not made up of parts. They are therefore removed from
true knowledge, which can only be of the absolute, which
has measure and limit.

As 'fallacy' is allied to 'ignorance', the antithesis to
'knowledge', it was natural that Plato, with his exalted
conception of φρόνησις, should devote much consideration
to a subject, on which few people now imagine that any

[1] p. 154. B. C.

uncertainty or difficulty can exist.[1] Thus in the *Philebus*[2] and the *Sophista*,[3] both of which dialogues are later than the *Theætetus*, he appears to have arrived at clearer views of the difference between Opinion and Knowledge. With the Megaric teachers, he saw that there was as essential a difference between intuitive reason and perception, as between right opinion and perfect intelligence. As μὴ ὄντα δοξάζειν is ψευδῆ δοξάζειν, but a man cannot think μὴ ὄντα, because whatever he thinks has a subjective existence to him, it follows that "false opinion" is an incorrect term, and one which should be eliminated from the vocabulary of dialecticians.

---

[1] Mr Campbell (Introd. p. lxxxi note) quotes from Descartes the proposition, "quod ad ideas spectat, si solae in se spectentur, *nec ad aliud quid illas referam*" (i.e. αἰσθήσει), "falsae proprie esse non possunt."

[2] p. 38. A.   [3] p. 263. E.

THEÆTETUS.

Euclides *and* Terpsio. (Scene, *at* Megara)

I. *Euclides.* Have you only just come from the country,
Terpsio, or have you been here some time?

Terpsio. A considerable time; and what is more, I have
been looking for you in the agora, and began to wonder that I
could not find you.

Euc. No wonder at all; the fact is, I was not in town.

Terp. Where were you, then?

Euc. I was going down to the harbour when I fell in with
Theætetus as they were carrying him from the camp at Corinth
towards Athens.

Terp. Alive, or dead?

Euc. Alive, and that is all: for he is in a very sad state B
from some wounds he has received; but worse than that, the
disorder that has broken out in the camp has been gradually
getting hold of him.

Terp. The dysentery, you mean?

Euc. Exactly.

Terp. What a hero we seem likely to lose if what you say
is true!

Euc. A fine lad and a brave one, Terpsio Indeed, it was
but just now that I heard some persons praising him warmly
for his conduct in the fight.[1]

Terp. There is nothing strange in that: it would be much
more surprising if he were not what they describe.   But how
is it that he did not stop here at Megara?   C

---

[1] The battle of Corinth, B.C. 392, between the Corinthians and Argives and
the Spartans.

Euc. He was anxious to get home; of course, I begged and advised him to stay; but he would not consent. So I went part of the way with him, and on returning I bethought myself of Socrates with feelings of wonder, for having spoken so like a prophet on many subjects, and especially about our young friend. If I mistake not, it was shortly before his death[1] that he met Theætetus, then a mere stripling; and after an interview and a conversation with him he expressed great admiration for his genius. When I came to Athens, he told me the subjects he had talked to him about, and well worth hearing they were. He also made the remark, 'That boy will D surely some day be distinguished, if he lives to be a man.'

Terp. And he spoke truly, as the result seems to show. But what was the subject of the conversation? Could you give me a full account of it?

Euc. No, certainly not, at least verbally, at the present moment. No! I made some notes of it for myself at the time on returning home, and afterwards recalled it to mind at leisure 143 and wrote it out. If there was any point I could not remember, I used to ask Socrates when I went to Athens, and then when I got back to Megara I made corrections; so that I now have pretty nearly the whole conversation written out.

Terp True; I heard you say so before. Indeed, I intended always to ask you to let me see it, but up to this time I have delayed doing so. But what prevents us from going through it now? Anyhow, I want a rest, having come all the way from the country.

Euc. For my own part, too, I may say that as I went with B Theætetus as far as the Fig-tree, I should not be sorry to rest. Let us therefore go to my house, and the boy shall read to us while we are taking our ease.

Terp. By all means.   [*They enter Euclides' house.*
Euc. Well then, Terpsio, here is the book I spoke of. I

---

[1] The power of prophecy was thought to be vouchsafed to great and good men when near dying

wrote the dialogue, you will understand, in this way: I did
not make Socrates describe to me how he held the conversation,
but I made him actually converse with the parties he named,[1]—
that is to say, with Theodore the geometer and our friend
Theætetus. In order therefore that in the writing of it I
might be spared the trouble of saying anything about the
persons between the speeches,—as about Socrates, whenever C
he spoke,[2] such as *Then I said*, or *Then I remarked*, or again,
about the respondent, as *He agreed*, or *He dissented from this*,
—to avoid these interruptions, I say, in my written account
Socrates himself is made to talk to the company, and I have
cut out such clauses as these.

Terp. And not without good precedent,[3] Euclides.

Euc Now, boy, take the book and read on.

[*Socrates is supposed to speak; the scene is at Athens.*]

II. *Socrates.* If, my Theodore, I cared more for Cyrene D
and the state of affairs there, I should ask about them and the
people, if you have any young men in your town who are
interested in geometry or any other branch of learning. But
I will not; I have a great regard for them, but more for those
here, and therefore I am the more anxious to know what young
men *we* have who are expected to make a figure. To this
subject then I not only direct my own attention, as far as I
can, but I make inquiry of others whenever I see our youths
willing to attend their instructions. Now you attract to your-

---

[1] The narrative is not διηγηματικὸς, (like the *Symposium*, for instance,) but
δραματικός. For ὡς διηγεῖτο I think we must read ὡς διελέγετο, and inf.
p 158 C., διαλέγεσθαι for διηγεῖσθαι

[2] περὶ αὐτοῦ seems to mean περὶ Σωκράτους, and καὶ ἐγὼ also means Socrates,
since Euclides is nowhere a speaker in the dialogue following. He appears
therefore at first to have contemplated writing Socrates' *own* account of what he
had said, and how Theodorus and Theætetus had answered him. The dialogue
that hence follows is strictly a *drama* of a past event.

[3] πρὸς τρόπου seems nearly the French *à la mode* The contrary, ἄπο
τρόπου, lit. ' different from the usual way,' is common enough in Plato, but is
rather variously rendered.

self more pupils than any one else, and with good reason, for you are held in esteem on other grounds beside your skill in geometry. So now, if you have met with any one worthy E of special mention, it would give me pleasure to hear it.

Theodore. Then, Socrates, it will be as much worth my while to tell you as yours to hear what a promising young fellow I have met with among your citizens. If, indeed, he were good-looking, I should feel some scruple at giving a description of him, lest a certain person should suspect I am an admirer of his; but as it is,—and you will pardon what I am going to say,—he is *not* handsome, but rather like you in his broad flat nose[1] and the external contour of the eyes; only he has these features less strongly marked than you have. So I have no fear in speaking of his other merits; for I assure 144 you that, of all I ever met with,—and I have conversed with very many,—I never found any one so favoured by nature and of so good a disposition. Indeed, he is surprisingly so; for that one who is quick at learning, to a degree that is seldom equalled,[2] should also be peculiarly gentle, and beside those qualities, as brave as any one,[3]—I should not have supposed was a thing possible; nor do I observe such results of education in any young men. No; your quick pupils, like our friend, who have their wits about them, and good memories, are usually hasty in their tempers;[4] they are carried along in an unsteady course like boats without ballast, and grow up

---

[1] σιμὸς is generally thought to describe a "snub" or "turned up" or "pug" nose. It is applied by Theocritus to the flatness of the bee's face in front, and properly expressed the satyr-like depression of the nose at the bridge, and its coming too close down to the mouth, with nostrils exposed and wide apart, πλατεῖα ῥὶς ἐπὶ χείλει, as Theocritus says of the Cyclops. The protuberance of the eye, or the *puffy* look round it, was regarded as a mark of sensuality. Hence κυλοιδιᾶν ὑπ᾽ ἔρωτος, Theoc i 38.

[2] Lit 'as is hard for another (to be)' Stallbaum quite misses the sense, *Sicuti alius difficilis solet esse istius modi homo.*

[3] *Magis quam quivis alius* —Stallbaum.

[4] Perhaps we should omit πρός. But the metaphor may be from the inclination of a scale to one side.

impulsive rather than of a manly decision. While your B
dullards, on the other hand, come reluctantly to their lessons,
and with nothing in their heads but forgetfulness. But our
young friend comes so smoothly and without the least hitch,[1]
with such success too, to his books and problems, and with the
greatest gentleness, like oil that makes no sound as it runs,
that one feels surprised that one so young can perform his
duties in so pleasing a way.

Soc. You give a promising account; but tell me further,
who of our citizens is his father?

Theo. I have heard his name, but don't recollect it. However, here he is between two friends coming this way. It C
seems that he and some of his companions have just been
getting rubbed with oil in the outer portico; and now, I suppose, they have been anointed and are coming this way. See
now, if you recognize him.

Soc. I know him. 'Tis the son of Euphronius of Sunium,
a character much as you describe your friend, and of general
good repute. If I mistake not, he left a very large property;
but the name of the youth I don't know.

Theo. His *name*, Socrates, is Theætetus. As for his fortune, D
I am afraid certain guardians of his have not improved it; yet
even in liberality in money matters one can't help admiring
him, Socrates.

Soc. 'Tis a generous fellow that you describe. Do oblige
me by asking him to take a seat here by me.

Theo. That shall be done.—Theætetus! come here and
speak to Socrates.

Soc. Yes, pray do, Theætetus, if only that I may get a
good sight of my own likeness; for Theodore tells me I have
a face like yours. Now suppose each of us had a lute, and he E
said they were both tuned to the same pitch; should we at
once believe him, or should we have considered whether the
man who says so skilled in music?

Theæt. We should have considered.

---

[1] Like the launching of a trireme from a well-greased slip

Soc. And if we found that he was, we should believe him; or, if ignorant of music, we should put no faith in him.

Theæt. True.

Soc. So now, I suppose, if we care at all about our faces being alike, we must consider whether the person who says so is conversant with lines,[1] or not.   145

Theæt I think he is that.

Soc. Has then Theodore any skill as a portrait painter?

Theæt. Not that I know of.

Soc. What! do you mean to say he is not even a geometer?[2]

Theæt. He is that, of course, Socrates.

Soc. Well, is he also versed in astronomy, and abstract calculation, and music, and such other kinds of knowledge as belong to general education?

Theæt. He appears to me to be so.

Soc. Then if he says we are like in any part of our bodies, either in praise or disparagement, we are by no means bound to listen to him.[3]

Theæt Perhaps not.

Soc. But what if he were to praise the *mind* of either of   B us, in respect of virtue and wisdom? Would it not be worth while for the party who heard the remark to take a little trouble to examine the person praised, and for him to exhibit himself freely and readily?

Theæt. Certainly it would, Socrates.

III. *Soc.* Then, my dear Theætetus, it is high time for you to exhibit and for me to observe. For I assure you, though Theodore has spoken favourably to me of very many, both strangers and citizens, he never praised any of them as he praised you.

---

[1] As a geometer. But it does not follow from his being γραφικὸς in this sense, that he is also ζωγραφικός.

[2] *i. e.* that he cannot even draw lines or circles The sense is, 'but surely, as a geometer, he must know how to draw.'

[3] If he is only generally clever, but has no special knowledge of portrait-painting.

Theæt. It might be right then to do as you say; only I am afraid he was not in earnest when he spoke of me thus.　　C

Soc. That is not Theodore's way; no, don't try to evade your promise by pretending that our friend here was only joking, or we may have to produce him in court as a witness. Whatever he says of you, no one will indict such a man for perjury. So take courage and abide by your agreement.[1]

Theæt. Well, I suppose I must do so, if you think it right.

Soc. Then tell me; you learn from Theodore, I presume, something about geometry?

Theæt. I do.

Soc. And also something of astronomy, music, and figures?

Theæt. I endeavour to do so, certainly.　　D

Soc. Well, and so do I, my child, from him at all events, if not from others, whom I may suppose to have any knowledge of these subjects. Still, though I have a fair acquaintance with them, there is one little matter[2] which I am in doubt about, and which I should like to consider with you and the present company. And now tell me; is not *learning* the becoming wiser in what one learns?

Theæt. Of course.

Soc. And it is in *wisdom* that the wise are wise.

Theæt. Yes.

Soc. Now, is there any difference between this and science?　E

Theæt. Of what do you speak?[3]

Soc. Wisdom. If we have accurate knowledge on any subjects, are we not also wise in them?

Theæt. Of course.

Soc. Then science and wisdom *are* the same.

Theæt. Yes.

Soc. This then is precisely the point that I am perplexed

---

[1] Expressed above by the words πάνυ μὲν οὖν.

[2] Ironical, this being in fact the subject of the dialogue, and one which from its difficulty is left undecided at the end. For ἔχω—σμικρὸν δέ τι we should perhaps read ἔχων—σμικρὸν ἔτι, etc.

[3] As τοῦτο might mean τὸ σοφώτερον γίγνεσθαι, an explanation is asked.

about, and unable to realise as I should wish in my own mind,
—*what* 'accurate knowledge' is.   Possibly now we may describe it.   What say you?   Which of you will be the first to 146
speak?   He who gives a wrong answer, and gets wrong
always, shall be Donkey (as the boys say who play at ball),
and have to sit down; while he who gets through the examination without a mistake, shall be King over us, and impose on
us any subject on which he may choose that we should give
answers.   Why are you silent?   I hope, Theodore, it is not
I that am acting the churl from fondness of discussion,[1] and in
my eagerness to make you converse, and so become friends and
have a chat with each other!

   Theodore.   That, Socrates, would be anything but churlish;   B
but desire one of these young men to give you a reply; for
I am not much used to this sort of conversation, and I am not
of an age either to become used to it.   But it will just suit
our young friends here, and they will greatly improve; for it
is quite true that youth has a capacity for improving in any
thing.   So, as you began, put the question to Theætetus, and
don't let him off.[2]

   Soc.   You hear, Theætetus, what Theodore says, and I suppose *you* will not care to disobey him, as, indeed, it is not   C
permitted for a younger man to do when a man learned in such
matters[3] gives his commands.   So let us have a good clear
answer without stint: what does 'Science' seem to you to be?

   Theæt.   Well, I suppose I must reply, Socrates, since you
and the rest desire me.   For of course, if I do make some
mistake, you will set me right.

   IV.   *Soc.*   Oh certainly,—that is, if we are able.

   Theæt.   Well, then, I think that what one can learn from
Theodore may be called sciences,—geometry and those you just

---

   [1] Socrates pretends that the answer is so obviously easy that any one of the
company could reply at once, if he chose.   Ironically he 'hopes he has said
nothing to offend,' and so to cause the silence of all.

   [2] As he had wished, sup. p. 145 B

   [3] Rather perhaps, 'it is not permitted in matters of this kind,' viz important
in their moral bearings and on Truth.

named[1], and again, shoe-making and the trades of the other D craftsmen, all and each of them, are nothing else than knowledge.

Soc. Like a generous and free-handed man, my friend, when asked for one you offer many,[2] and various for simple.

Theæt. What do you mean by that, Socrates?

Soc. It has no meaning, perhaps; but what I think I intended to say, I will explain. When you speak of a cobbler's art, do you mean by it anything else than the science of the manufacture of shoes?

Theæt. Nothing else.

Soc. Well, when you speak of carpentry, is it of anything E but the science of manufacturing wooden implements?

Theæt. My reply is the same in this case too.

Soc. Then in both you confine your answer to that, of which each art is the science?

Theæt. Yes.

Soc. But, my Theætetus, the question asked was not this, of what things 'Knowledge' is the science, nor how many sciences there are. For it was not with any wish to *count* them that we asked, but to get a clear knowledge about science, what it is in the abstract. Or is there nothing at all in what I say?

Theæt. Indeed, you say very rightly.

Soc. Now then consider well what I am going further to remark. Supposing a person should ask us about some commonplace and obvious thing, for instance, What is clay? should we 147 not appear ridiculous if we answered him, 'Clay is the clay of the potters, and also of the porcelain-makers, and of the brickmakers likewise'?

Theæt. Perhaps we should.

Soc. In the first place, I presume, in supposing that the questioner would understand what clay was from our answer,

---

[1] Astronomy, music, etc , p. 145. D.

[2] Specific examples instead of an abstraction or generality.

' Clay is clay,'—adding either ' such as the image-makers use,'
or any other artists you please.   Or do you believe that a man
understands the name of a thing, if he does not know what the   B
thing itself is ?

Theæt   By no means.

Soc.   Then one who does not know what *science* means,
cannot understand either the ' science of shoes.'

Theæt   He cannot.

Soc.   And again, whoever is ignorant what science is, does
not comprehend the knowledge of leather, or any other trade

Theæt.   That is so.

Soc.   Then the answer is absurd, when a man is asked
' What is knowledge ?' if he gives in reply the name of some
trade.   For his answer is confined to the knowledge of some
particular subject ; but he was not asked *that*.   C

Theæt.   So it seems

Soc.   Thus then, when he might, I suppose, have answered
in a common way, and in brief, he goes a roundabout way that
has no end to it.   For instance, in the question about clay, it
was obvious, surely, and simple to reply, that ' earth mixed up
with any fluid would be clay ',[1] and you need not concern
yourself as to *whose* clay it is.

V.   *Theæt.*   Yes, it appears easy enough *now*, Socrates,
when you put it thus.   But your question seems like one
which lately presented itself to us when we were talking,—
I and your namesake here, Socrates.   D

Soc.   What was that, now, Theætetus?

Theæt   Theodore here was writing down for us some facts
about the powers[2] of numbers, and showing us that a rectangle

---

[1] A curious instance of the total ignorance of chemistry in Plato's age. Not
only does the same word express ' mud' and ' clay,' but Plato supposes the constituents are precisely the same

[2] *Roots*, we should now say.   He means, literally, the equivalence of certain
numbers expressing the sides of a rectangle, with the superficial feet they represent.   The ' square of a number' assumes both sides of the rectangle to be the
same , *e g* $4 \times 4 = 16$, means that 4, if it has another 4 making a rectangle,
gives 16 superficial feet.

composed of a three-foot and a five-foot line (3×5) is not geometrically commensurable by the one-foot line[1]; and so he went on taking examples one by one up to the seventeen-foot line; and at that he stopped.[2] The idea then occurred to us, that as these powers seemed indefinitely numerous, we should try to comprehend them under some one general term by which we might describe all those of this kind.

Soc. Did you then find such a term?

Theæt I think we did; but consider it also yourself.

Soc. Tell me then.

Theæt. We divided all number into two kinds[3] That which could be resolved into an equal number of factors we compared to a figure square in form, and called it both quadrangular and equal-sided.

Soc. And very appropriately too.

Theæt. Well, the intervening numbers, such as three and five, and all such as cannot be resolved into equal factors, but can only become either more taken fewer times, or less taken more times,[4] and so, do as you will, must ever be inclosed by one side that is greater than another side,—this kind of numbers we compared to the oblong form, and called it 'Long number.'

E

148

---

[1] Because one line has only *three*, and the other line has *five* ποδιαῖαι In other words, this rectangle would not form a square, but a long-shaped parallelogram, and therefore arithmetically the product, $3 \times 5 = 15$ would be a surd and the square root could not be extracted. This square *root* is the briefest way of expressing the size meant, *e. g.* a square constructed on a given line of four feet contains $4 \times 4 = 16$ superficial square feet

[2] Rectangles of 5×7, 7×9, 9×11, etc.

[3] *i.e.* square numbers and surds. The number 16 can be represented by 4×4, as well as by 2×8. But *twelve*, though equivalent to 2×6 or 3×4, cannot be made up of equal factors The first represents a square, the other an unequal-sided parallelogram. You cannot have a square containing twelve superficial feet, though twelve is an equal number

[4] Say, either 6×2 or 2×6 Geometrically, 'a parallelogram standing on its end or laid on its side,' as it were. When we say we cannot extract the square root of 15, we mean that 15 superficial feet cannot be packed in a square figure, but only in a figure whose rectangle is 3×5 or 5×3

Soc. Very good indeed. But what next?

Theæt. All the lines which make up an equilateral rect-angular superficial area, we distinguished as 'regular,' and all that include a parallelogram, as 'powers', on the ground that in linear figure they were not commensurable with those other lines,[1] but only with the superficial squares they were equi-valent to. And similarly with cube numbers.   B

Soc. None could possibly have done better, my dear boys; so that Theodore, as it seems to be, will not be held liable to the penalties of perjury.[2]

Theæt. But, Socrates, your question about knowledge I am not likely to answer as readily as that about the geometrical extension and the power of number, though it seems to me that you require some such a reply. I am afraid therefore that if Theodore was right in the other matter, he is wrong in this.[3]

Soc. What! Suppose that, in praising you for running,   C he had said, 'I never met with any young man so good a runner,' and then, in running a race, you had been beaten by one who was in the very prime of his strength, and had no superior in speed, do you think our friend would have praised you the less truly for that?[4]

Theæt. No, I do not.

Soc. But now about this knowledge,—as I was saying just now,—do you suppose it is a small matter to find out what it is, and not rather the part of very close thinkers?[5]

Theæt. Indeed, I think it is a task of quite first-rate men.[5]

Soc. Then have confidence about yourself, and believe

---

[1] Both of which were *equal*.

[2] Since he praised you justly.

[3] In praising me for aptitude in matters beside geometry. See p. 144. A.

[4] It did not follow, because he praised you, that no one was *superior* to you; and therefore he cannot be said to have spoken falsely. He spoke the truth according to his knowledge.

[5] There seems no necessity to alter ἀκριβῶν into ἄκρων, which Stallbaum edits from the inferior MSS. Either gives a good sense, however.

there is something in what Theodore says, and endeavour by D every means in your power to get information about knowledge, among other things, and the true nature of it.

Theæt. As far as painstaking is concerned, Socrates, it shall be found out.

VI. *Soc.* Come, then, as you have just given a good example of your skill, so try to imitate the answer you gave about the powers of numbers, and as you comprehended them, numerous though they were, under one head, so also endeavour to call the various kinds of knowledge by some one term.

Theæt. I assure you, Socrates, I have many, many times E undertaken the consideration of this question, on hearing the answers that were brought away from you; but alas! I am neither able to convince myself that I give any satisfactory account of it, nor to hear any one else giving it in the way that you recommend;[1] and yet, on the other hand, I cannot altogether resign my interest in the subject.

Soc. The fact is, my dear Theætetus, you are in travail; you are not empty-pated, but have conceived something in that brain of yours.

Theæt. I don't know, Socrates. I only describe what I feel.

Soc. And do you mean to say, you ridiculous fellow, you 149 have never heard that I am the son of a cross-faced old lady,[2] Phaenarete?

Theæt. Well, I have heard that before now.

Soc. And have you heard also that I practice the same art?

Theæt. Certainly not.

Soc. But I can assure you I do; but don't tell of me to the other professors, for they are not aware that I have this faculty. And so, in their ignorance, they do not say this of me, but

---

[1] By *synthesis*, or classification.

[2] Of course, γενναίας is a joke on a somewhat humble though useful profession. By βλοσυρᾶς, 'frightful' (Hom *Il.* vii. 212, Æsch. *Suppl.* 813, *Eum.* 161), the alarm of young wives at the sight of the midwife may be meant Aristophanes seems to allude to Socrates' mother in *Ach.* 49 and *Nub* 137.

only that I am the strangest of men, and drive people into perplexities. Have you heard *that* about me?

Theæt. I certainly have.　　　　　　　　　　　　　　B

Soc. Must I tell you the reason, then?

Theæt. By all means.

Soc. Consider now the whole case of these midwives, and you will more easily perceive my meaning. You are aware, of course, that none of them while she is herself having a family, acts as midwife to others, but only those who are now too old to have offspring.

Theæt. Certainly.

Soc. And the reason of this, as men say, is that Artemis, without being a mother herself, has the office of bringing children into the world.[1] Now she does not permit women who have never borne children to act as midwives to others, because human nature is too weak to undertake the practice of anything of which it has had no experience. Therefore she assigned this duty only to those who are too old to have children, paying this compliment to her own likeness to them [2]　　　C

Theæt. Perhaps that is so.

Soc. Then is not this not only probable, but a matter of course,—that women who are pregnant or not pregnant are more surely known by midwives than by any others?

Theæt. Certainly.

Soc. And these same midwives by giving drugs and using charms are able to bring on the birth-pains, or, if they choose, to make them more endurable; also to cause those who are in difficult labour to give the child birth, or, if it should be agreed to procure abortion of the fœtus, then they can effect that.　　　D

Theæt. All that is true.

Soc. Have you ever noticed this other office of theirs,— that they are matchmakers[3] of the greatest skill, as being very

---

[1] She is λοχία θεὸς, but, as a virgin, herself ἄνευ λοχείας, or ἀνειλείθυια, Eur. *Ion.* 453.

[2] Both being ἄνευ λοχείας, though from different causes.

[3] Our word does not express προμνήστρια. The Greeks, who thought so

clever at forming an opinion what kind of man and woman must consort together to produce the finest children?

Theæt. I certainly am not aware of that at all.

Soc. Then let me tell you that they pique themselves more on this than on the surgical operation. For observe: would **E** you say it belonged to the same, or to a different art, to grow and gather in the fruits of the earth, and also to know on what soil what trees and what seeds must be planted?

Theæt. Not to a different, but to the same art.

Soc. Do you suppose then that in the case of a woman[1] the judgment in question is one art, and the bringing of the child into the world is another?

Theæt. Why it does not seem likely.

Soc. Of course not. But the fact is, it is through that **150** dishonest traffic, which requires no skill at all, of procuring a meeting between a man and a woman, (which, as we all know, is called the trade of the procuress,) that your midwives, as having a proper pride, shun the practice of giving advice about marriages, fearing lest through this latter profession they should incur the odium of practising the former. For, of course, none but real midwives are entitled to give a sound opinion on such subjects.

Theæt. So it seems.

Soc What the midwives do, then, I have said; but it is less than the part that I play. For it is not in the nature of

---

much of physical beauty, consulted these women professionally as to the probability of offspring being born of a fine type and constitution. See Ar *Nub* 41.

εἶθ᾽ ὤφελ᾽ ἡ προμνήστρι᾽ ἀπολέσθαι κακῶς,
ἥτις με γῆμαι 'πῆρε τὴν σὴν μητέρα.

It may well seem surprising to us that a professed teacher of high virtue and morality should have held such a conversation as the following with a young and ingenuous lad. Still more surprising is the free way in which Socrates enters into these delicate topics with a lady, in *Sympos.* p. 201. D. seqq. Whether he held them or not, his admirer Plato does not scruple to attribute to him such kind of talk.

[1] Lit. τοῦ τοιούτου, τουτέστι σπείρειν εἰς, etc. The figure of speech is common, *e.g.* Pind. *Pyth.* iv. 255, Soph *Ant.* 569.

women to bring forth sometimes mere semblances,[1] at other B
times genuine offspring, and that without any means of distinguishing them. If it were so, there would be no greater or
more honourable duty for midwives than to separate the true
and the false. Do you not think so?

Theæt. I do.

VII. *Soc.* Well, *my* art of midwifery has all the duties
attached to it which theirs has, but it differs in this, that I
deliver men and not women, and look to their minds when
there is anything to come from them, and not to their bodies.
But the chief boast of *our* art is this, that it can put to the
test in every way and ascertain whether it is a mere sham and C
a delusion that the ideas of the young man are giving birth to,
or a true and genuine sentiment. *This* peculiarity, I grant,
belongs to me as well as to midwives;—I have never given
birth to any wisdom[2]; and the taunt that many have before
now uttered against me is quite true,—that I put questions to
others, but never give an answer myself on any subject from
having nothing clever to say. Well, the reason of this I will
explain. The god constrains me to play the part of midwife
to others, but does not allow me to have a family myself.[3] I
am then on my own part anything but wise, for I have no
such great results to show as any offspring of my genius that D
has seen the light. But, although those who converse with
me seem at first to be, in some cases, even wholly ignorant,
yet all, as our intercourse goes on,—that is, to whom the god
permits it,—show a marvellous improvement, as both they and
others imagine; and it is also evident, that this improvement
is not due to anything they have ever learnt from me, but

---

[1] Alluding, perhaps, to the story of Stesichorus about the wraith of Helen.
See *Respubl.* p. 586. C. For τοῦτο δὲ just below we should perhaps read
ταῦτα δέ.

[2] He alludes probably to his not having written any books, which are sometimes spoken of by Plato as παῖδες and γεννήματα.

[3] There seems a playful allusion to the oracular warning given to Laius,
not to beget children.

comes from the many fine ideas they have hit upon and retained
in their own imaginations. But then the safe delivery of
these conceptions is due to me and the god. And this is how
we know it: many 'ere now have not been aware of our part
in the matter, but have thought it was all due to them-   E
selves, and so, despising me in their own hearts, or induced
by others to do so, they have left me sooner than they ought,
and thus, from keeping bad company, have not only brought
to an untimely birth the other notions they had conceived, but
have lost, from bad nursing, those which I had assisted
them in bringing into the world, and that because they valued
mere shams and semblances more than the truth. Thus in the
end they seem both to themselves and to others to be utterly
illiterate. One of these is Aristides, the son of Lysimachus; 151
and there are very many more. Now, when such persons
come back to me, wanting me to converse with them, and
having recourse to all sorts of strange expedients,[1] the Familiar
that ever attends me prevents me from having any more to say
to some of these, while it allows me to keep company with
others: and then they again begin to improve of themselves.[2]
There is another point in which my pupils resemble women in
labour: they are in travail and are filled with restless longings
by night and by day even more than those of the other sex;
and these labour-pains my skill can bring on or alleviate.
So much then for these. But some there are, my Theætetus,   B
who seem to me not to have an idea in them; and well knowing that they do not require *my* aid, I act the part of a friend
in making other matches for them;[3] and (to speak under favour
of the god) I can make a pretty good guess at the sort of

---

[1] Like ardent lovers in trying to win the objects of their affection Socrates
ironically describes some conceited pupils who have been enticed away by the
Sophists, and whom he will only take back again on their showing real signs of
earnestness and good ability.

[2] He had said before, παρ' ἐμοῦ οὐδὲν μαθόντες.

[3] Lit. 'Those who may have appeared to me not to have an idea in them, I
good-naturedly find other partners for,' etc., i e. I send them to other teachers

teachers by whose conversation they will be benefited. Many of them I have made over to Prodicus[1], and many to other wise and inspired teachers.—If I have made a long story, my good friend, it was on this account; I suspected that you,—as indeed you imagine yourself,—were in travail with some notion that you had conceived in your mind. Now, therefore, behave towards me as to the son of a midwife who himself knows something of the art; and do your best to answer such C questions as I may put to you If, on examining what you say, I shall consider it a mere sham and not a reality, and so try to remove and reject it, do not be savage with me as women are about their first offspring. For I can tell you that many have shown such a temper towards me as to be quite ready to bite me when I propose to rid them of some nonsensical idea. They fancy that I am not acting kindly in doing this; they are yet very far from understanding that, as no god bears any ill will to man, so I do nothing of this sort from unkindness; D it is because it is not permitted me[2] to concede falsehood or to put out of sight the truth.

VIII. Try, therefore, Theætetus, to begin again and say what you consider *knowledge* to be. And don't tell me that you can't; if the god wills, and you play the man, you will find yourself able.

Theæt Well, Socrates, when *you* so encourage me to try, it would be a shame not to do one's very best to say what one has to say.[3] I think, then, that if a man *knows* anything, he E has a perception of it; and so—according to my present view, —*knowledge* is nothing else than *perception.*[4]

[1] The metaphor from sexual union is kept up in ἐξέδωκα, which is sometimes used of making over a mistress to another. There is much dry humour in speaking thus of pupils who in their conceit have left Socrates for the more pretentious instructions of a sophist.

[2] As the servant of Apollo, ἀψευδὴς θεός. There are few nobler sentiments than that contained in the brief words—ψεῦδος ξυγχωρῆσαι καὶ ἀληθὲς ἀφανίσαι οὐδαμῶς ΘΕΜΙΣ   [3] Perhaps τρόπῳ is an interpolation

[4] It is this old and obvious, but inaccurate definition that Plato undertakes to disprove in the present dialogue.

Soc. Well said, and right nobly, my boy! That is just as one ought to speak who wishes to say without any reserve what he really thinks. But come, now, let us consider the matter in common, to see if our egg has a chick in it, or is a mere wind-egg. *Perception,* you say, is knowledge?

Theæt. I do.

Soc. Indeed, you seem to have delivered an opinion about 152 knowledge that is by no means common-place: for it is one that Protagoras also gave, though it was in a somewhat different way that he expressed the same meaning. If I mistake not, he says that 'Man is the measure of all things,'—of things that are, that they are so, and of non-existing things that they are not. You have read it, I think?

Theæt. I have read it many times.

Soc. Does he not then say, in effect, that as things appear severally to me, such they are to me, and as they seem to you, to you they are : and both of us, I suppose, are human beings.[1]

Theæt. Well, he does say so.

Soc. And we may be sure that a wise man is not in the   B habit of talking nonsense. Let us therefore follow him in his argument. Does it not happen sometimes, when the wind blows, that one of us feels cold, another does not? And one feels it but slightly, another very much?

Theæt. Certainly.

Soc. Must we then on that particular occasion say that the wind is cold of itself,[2] or not cold? Or must we accept the

---

[1] And therefore satisfy the terms of the saying, μέτρον ἄνθρωπος. The same proposition in effect is expressed by three formulas, (1) αἴσθησις ἐπιστήμη, Theætetus, (2) πάντων μέτρον ἄνθρωπος, Protagoras; (3) πάντα ῥεῖ, Homer and Heraclitus Plato's object is to show that there must be a truth and a reality more true and more permanent than these dogmas imply ; and hence his view of ἰδέαι, eternal and unchangeable, as contrasted with merely phenomenal, existences.

[2] *i. e* independently of the man who feels it so, or absolutely and not merely relatively cold The argument brought to bear against the definition of Theætetus is, that what you *perceive* has no real existence, since it is only a γένεσις to *you.*

view of Protagoras, that to the man who shivers it is cold, but him who does not, it is not cold?

Theæt. That is probable.

Soc. Then it also *seems* so to each of them?

Theæt. Yes.

Soc. And this words 'seems' is perceiving.

Theæt. It is so.

Soc. Then fancy and perception are the same,[1] at least in   C feelings of heat and all sensations of that kind. For just as each person feels them, such, as it seems, they are to each.

Theæt. Likely enough.

Soc. Then perception must always be of something that exists; and it cannot be mistaken, since it is exact science.

Theæt. It seems so.

Soc. Then, in the name of all that is elegant and refined,[2] was not Protagoras a truly wise man when he gave us, who are but the rabble multitude, a mere hint of this beautiful doctrine, but told his disciples the whole truth under the seal of secresy?[3]

Theæt. In what sense do you say this, Socrates?   D

Soc. I will tell you a doctrine of no common-place kind. Nothing exists singly and by itself, and you cannot rightly call anything of itself by any name[4]; but if you speak of it as

[1] This ingenious paradox is deduced directly from the premises, and is such a result as at once to throw a doubt on the proposition that αἴσθησίς is ἐπιστήμη. In what follows, we should probably read ἔν γε θερμοῖς for ἔν τε, etc.

[2] He must have been one of those known as οἱ χαρίεντες, sometimes mentioned by Aristotle as good judges of moral questions.

[3] The distinction of esoteric and exoteric doctrines came, in all probability, from the Eleusinian mysteries, and it prevailed largely not only in the philosophical schools but with the early Christians. The reserve in teaching (*oeconomia* or *arcani disciplina*, the 'learning how to keep a secret') was due to that fear of violating some hidden mystery which seems common to all ancient forms of religion. See Pind. *Ol.* ii. 17; Hor. *Od.* iii. 2. 25, 'est et fideli tuta silentio merces.'

[4] Everything is but relative, and has no absolute existence. There must be *two* (patient and agent) in every sensation; *e. g.* there can be no such a thing as colour without an eye to see it, or bitterness without a tongue to feel it.

great, it will seem under other conditions to be small; if heavy, also light; and so with everything else, on the ground of there being no *single* existence either as a thing or as a quality. The things we now speak of as existing, using thereby an incorrect expression, are really produced from change of position and motion and union of one with another; for nothing ever *is*; it is ever being produced. On this point all philosophers ranged together, Parmenides excepted, agree; E Protagoras following Heraclitus, and Empedocles,[1]—as well as the great composers of each kind of poetry, Epicharmus of comedy, Homer of tragedy. For Homer, in saying—

'Ocean, from whom the gods were created, and Tethys their mother,'[2]

has in effect declared that all things are produced from flux and movement. Does he not seem to you to mean this?

Theæt. He does.

IX. *Soc.* Then no one surely, in joining issue with so 153 numerous a host with Homer for their leader, can hope to escape ridicule

Theæt. It would not be easy, Socrates.

Soc. No, indeed, Theætetus. For the following facts are sufficient proofs of the proposition, that what seems to exist, but is really production, is caused by motion, and non-exist-ence or dissolution by rest,—heat and fire, which, as we all know, both generates and rears everything else, is itself pro-duced from motion[3] and friction, and this is a kind of movement. Are not these the processes by which fire is kindled?

---

[1] The reading of the Bodleian, ξυμφέρεσθον, may be defended, if the dual be regarded as expressing two in particular, i. e. Protagoras and Heraclitus con-ceived as one (which is the force of τε καὶ), and Empedocles. A precisely similar passage is Pindar, Ol. ii. 87, where the dual γαρυέτον is used after the plural μαθόντες to indicate that Bacchylides and Simonides are meant.

[2] *Iliad* xiv 201. There is probably an ironical allusion to the mystical school of interpreters, who regarded Homer as the originator of all wisdom and philosophy.

[3] Properly, φορὰ is 'motion in space,' like that of the planets; κίνησις is ' movement from a state of inertia.' Here, as in so many of the speculations of

Theæt. Certainly they are.   B

Soc. But surely also animals of all kinds are generated by the same processes ?[1]

Theæt. Of course they are.

Soc Well, is not the *condition*[2] of all living bodies impaired by quietness and inactivity, but kept up for long by exercises and movements?

Theæt. Certainly.

Soc. And surely it is by learning and practice, which are stirrings of the mind, that the habit formed in the soul[3] both acquires new information and retains it and becomes improved, while by lying by, which is non-practice and non-learning, it not only does not learn anything, but even forgets what it has learnt?   C

Theæt. Assuredly so.

Soc. Then the one of these, motion, is a good in respect to both soul and body, and the other is the contrary?

Theæt. It seems so.

Soc. Need I then further speak of lulls and calms and things of that kind, and say that states of rest sap and destroy, while the contrary conditions preserve? and beside these, as the final argument,[4] shall I leave you no escape in bringing you over to my view, but assert that Homer means nothing else by his 'golden chain' than the sun,—in a word, that he means to show that so long as the revolving motion of the   D heaven is kept up, and the sun, all things are maintained

the ancient philosophers, we have the first glimpse of a most important scientific fact   Heat, force, molecular motion, vital energy, are conditions or manifestations of matter, which is never really at rest.

[1] τρῖψις and φορὰ (the *sustentatio*) are used here in the sexual sense. Applied to fire, τρῖψις is the rubbing two pieces of wood till they break into flame, or the use of flint and steel, etc

[2] ἕξις is here emphatic, as distinguished from γένεσις. In the same way ψυχὴ is opposed to σώματα just below.

[3] There is a play on the literal and the derivative senses of ἕξις, 'the holding' and the 'state' or 'condition.' Properly, κτᾶσθαι precedes ἔχειν, as inf. p 197. B.

[4] It seems best to take τὸν κολοφῶνα as an accusative in apposition to the sentence.

in their existence both among gods and men; whereas, if this were to come to a stand, as if bound fast, all things would come to ruin, and there would ensue what is described by the proverb, 'all topsy-turvy '¹

Theæt. To me, Socrates, Homer does seem to express just what you say.

X. *Soc.* Then, my excellent friend, view the matter in this light:—first, with respect to sight, that which you call *white* does not exist *per se* as something external to your eyes, nor is it *in* your eyes. Do not therefore assign any place   E to it at all; for it would at once be in existence, if it were somewhere in position; and it would be permanent, and not always in course of being produced

Theæt. Then how should I speak of it?

Soc. Let us follow our late argument, and assume that nothing exists as a *one* by itself. Thus black and white and any other colour you please will be found to be produced by the eye being directed to the object with the kind of motion that suits that organ²; and thus what we call *colour* of any 154 kind will not be the object that strikes nor the eye that is struck, but an intermediate effect brought into existence for the particular person at the time.³ Or would you insist that what seems any colour to you, is also the same to a dog or to any creature?

¹ In ἄνω κάτω there is an allusion to the Homeric story of men trying to pull down the gods, and the gods pulling up men, earth and all, by the chain, *Il.* viii. 17, etc.

² Reflection from a surface coming to the eye, taste to tongue, smell to nose, etc., produce results in us. Whereas, if the nose met light, or the eye met smell, no effect at all would be produced. It would be as barren as the union of two animals of different genus

³ This is strictly true. Colour is only the effect of a molecular arrangement of matter which resolves the spectrum and reflects a certain ray An object is only coloured to the person who sees it, *i. e.* there must be an eye by which the effect of light is perceived. It does not *remain* coloured when the eye is withdrawn. So sugar is not sweet, pepper is not pungent, unless there is a palate or a nose to act upon. Both are effects of molecular action on sentient nerves.

Theæt. Indeed I would not.

Soc. Well, does anything seem the same to another *man*[1] as it does to you? Are you quite sure of this, or is it not much rather the case that it does not seem the same even to yourself, through your never being in precisely the same bodily condition?

Theæt. This seems to me to be the case rather than that.

Soc. Then if any object by which we compare our own stature, or which we lay hold of, were really great, or really hot, it would not, by comparison with another thing, become different,—that is, of course, so long as it admitted no change in itself.[2] And again, if that which measures itself or which touches something else had possessed any of these qualities absolutely, it never would have become different if another object had been brought to it or in some way altered,[3] while the original object remained unchanged. As we now use terms, my friends, we are compelled in a careless easy way to say what is not only surprising, but ridiculous,[4] as Protagoras would assert, and any one who essays to use the same course of reasoning that he does. B

Theæt. How? What reasoning do you mean?

Soc. Take a small matter as an example, and you will understand my meaning fully. Suppose you place four dice near to six others. Then, of course, we say six are more than four, and half as many again. But if you put twelve dice, then six are fewer and only half the number. And we are obliged to use this language. Would *you* for a moment allow any other? C

[1] Opposed to ὁτφοῦν ζώφ.

[2] All qualities are relative, not absolute. A white wall might seem dingy by fresh snow; one pole would seem tall compared with another, but short compared with a third, etc.

[3] A piece sawn off one of two posts might make the other post (relatively) tall instead of short.

[4] That things are at once tall and short, hot and cold, etc., though they undergo no change in themselves. By the use of any term implying *existence* this anomaly is incurred. We should use γίγνεται, not ἔστι.

Theæt. Not I, indeed.

Soc. Well, now, if Protagoras should ask you, or any one else, Can a thing, Theætetus, possibly become greater or more in any other way than by increase, what answer will you give?

Theæt. Why, Socrates, if I answer what I think in reference to the question just put, I should say it is not possible; but if in reference to the former question about the dice, then, guarding my reply against contradiction, I should say it *is* possible.   D

Soc. By Hera, a clever and oracular answer, my friend! But it seems to me that if you say it is possible, a case will occur like that in the play of Euripides,—your language will be consistent, but your mind will still be open to conviction.[1]

Theæt. True

Soc Then if you and I were clever and wise, and had investigated all the phenomena in psychology, we might now, and for the rest of the argument, by way of pastime try each other's prowess, by engaging like sophists in a contest of this   E kind, and parry statement by statement. But, as we are not sophists, but ordinary men, we will endeavour first to get a clear view of the facts themselves,[2] and what meaning we attach to them,—whether we find they can be reconciled with one another, or not at all.

Theæt. Indeed, that is precisely what I should myself desire.

XI. *Soc.* And so should I. And this being the case, shall we not now quite at our leisure, as having plenty of time at our disposal, again reconsider the matter, not in a   155 spirit of peevishness, but really to put our own convictions to the test, and find out what these visionary notions in us are. In looking at the first, we shall say, I suppose that 'Nothing can ever become greater or less, either in bulk or in number, so long as it retains its own size.' Is it not so?[3]

---

[1] You will say so, but not really think so.

[2] *i. e.* your views compared with my views, apart from the λόγοι or statements of them

[3] This will hold as an absolute truth, but not when applied relatively, as to the numbers of dice.

Theæt. It is.

Soc. The second proposition is, 'What has nothing added to it and nothing taken away, neither increases nor diminishes, but is always the same in size.'

Theæt. Undoubtedly.

Soc. Is there not then yet one more case; 'What was not   B before, but afterwards is, must have become so, and undergone a process of becoming.'

Theæt. I should think that is true.

Soc. Well, now, these three propositions, as accepted by us, are at variance with each other in our minds, when we bring forward the case of the dice, or when we say that I, who am of a certain stature, without having grown or become less, in one year am first taller than you who are young, and then shorter, without my proper height having had anything taken off it, but simply because you have grown. For 'I am after-   C wards what before I was not, without having become so.' For without *becoming* it is impossible to *have become;* and if I lost nothing of my bulk, I never could have gone through the process of *becoming* less. There are countless other cases of the same kind, if, I suppose, we are to accept these views. You follow me, I think, Theætetus? You seem, indeed, to me to be very well versed in such inquiries.

Theæt. I protest, Socrates, I am filled with exceeding wonder at these conclusions, and sometimes, when I look steadily at them, I seem to reel, as if darkness were coming over my sight.

Soc. Ah! Theodore, my friend, seems to have made a fair   D guess at your disposition. This feeling of wonder is very characteristic of your philosopher: indeed, that and nothing but that is the source of all philosophy, and the poet who said that Iris was the daughter of Thaumas[1] seems to have been an adept in genealogy. But do you now begin to see *why* these

---

[1] Hesiod, *Theog.* 780. Hence Ovid calls her *Thaumantias, (Fasti).* Plato rightly says that the origin of all inquiry and observation is the feeling, 'I wonder *why* this is.' Cicero also says that 'the beginning of philosophy is ignorance (*De Nat. D. init.*).

things are so, from the doctrines we attribute to Protagoras, or are you still in doubt?

Theæt. I don't quite see it as yet.

Soc. Will you thank me then if I help you to investigate the true meaning, concealed as it is from the many, of the   E views held by a man, or rather by men,[1] of note?

Theæt. Of course I shall thank you, and very heartily too.

XII. *Soc.* Then look round you in every direction, lest some of the uninitiated should overhear us. These are the people who do not believe in the existence of anything but what they can clutch in their hands,[2] and do not admit in the category of Being natural operations or creations or any unseen agency.

Theæt. In truth, Socrates, they are a hard and unim-   156 pressible set that you speak of.[3]

Soc. They are, indeed, my son, an illiterate lot. But there are others much more subtle in language,[4] whose mystical doctrines I am about to describe. And the leading principle, on which all the theories we have just mentioned depend, is this,—that Motion is everything, and beside that nothing else is.[5] Of this motion there are two kinds, each infinite in its manifestations, the one having the faculty of acting, the other

---

[1] Since Heraclitus' doctrine of flux is virtually the same as Protagoras' μέτρον, both alike implying non-existence (negative of οὐσία). There is an allusion in ἀλήθεια to the title of Protagoras' book, and in ἀποκεκρυμμένην to the doctrine of reserve, ἀπόρρητον.

[2] The 'giants' who grasped stones and sticks in their war against the gods (*Sophist* p 246—7).

[3] A metaphor from an anvil from which the hammer recoils without leaving a mark. Some objectors to Plato's doctrine of ἰδέαι or Abstracts must be meant; but it is not certain to what school he specially points   Plato appears to have been 'touchy', and intolerant both of men and opinions where they differed from himself

[4] Antisthenes is probably meant, the founder of, or predecessor to, the Cynics.

[5] A profound view of Cosmogony, and one recognised by modern science,— given only Matter, or 'Cosmic vapour,' to be acted upon, and a *principle* or *cause* of motion, and you have worlds and all that is in or on them.

of being acted on. Well, from the union and close contact of
these with each other offspring is produced, also infinite in its
number of forms, but again of two kinds,—one the sensible,   B
the other sense,—that is, a power of perception which always
is produced along with the object of sense, and is born at the
same instant with it.¹ Now the senses we express by such
terms as these: we call them acts of seeing, hearing, smelling,
besides feelings of cold or heat, even the emotions of pleasure
and pain, or desire and fear; and though there are endless
varieties of these which have no names at all, yet those which
have names are very numerous. Now the class of phenomena
which we speak of as objects of sense are produced simultaneously with each of the senses,—colours of all kinds for
different sorts of eye-sight, and in the same way sounds for   C
hearing, and the other sensuous effects that are produced by
a simultaneous birth with the other senses. Now, what has
this story² to do with our former inquiries? Do you understand?

Theæt. I can't say that I do, Socrates.

Soc. Then attend, and we will see if we can arrive at a
conclusion. The import of the argument is this: that all things
with which we are conversant have motion, but in that motion
there is sometimes speed and sometimes slowness.³ Now the

---

¹ *e. g.* the faculty of seeing when some object is presented to the eye.

² There is a little irony in the evasion of the more natural word λόγος,
'statement' or 'account'.

³ Light, for instance, travels with extreme velocity, sound somewhat slowly.
Hence light going to eye, and sound to ear, each having a course peculiar
to itself, produce results or effects which are not the same in the time of their
production. (See Ar. *Eth Nic.* x. iii. § 4.) One kind of κίνησις is ἀλλοίωσις,
'alteration', *e. g.* the gradual fading of colour; and Socrates perhaps contrasts
this with actual motion or change of position, ἐν φορᾷ. Or again, he may refer
to law (πέρας) impressed on matter (ἄπειρον), *i. e.* that a limitation to indefinite
motion is the cause of creation. The whole passage is, no doubt, purposely
obscure. The terms used, γεννᾶν, πλησιάζειν, are evidently borrowed from
sexual union. Perhaps we should read thus· ὅσον μὲν οὖν βραδὺ. ἐν τῷ αὐτῷ
τὴν κίνησιν ἴσχει, καὶ οὕτω δὴ γεννᾷ· [ὅσον δὲ ταχὺ,] πρὸς τὰ πλησιάζοντα· τὰ
δὲ γεννώμενα οὕτω δὴ θάττω ἐστί. These words would well describe the

slow kind of movement takes place without change of position, and produces its results in this way; [that which has speed,] has a real motion towards the sentient faculties which will admit of a union,[1] and the results so produced are quicker; for they have motion in space, and their movement is naturally one of change in position. Thus, when the eye, and any other object suited to the nature of that organ, unite and produce whiteness, and a perception of whiteness coincident and congenial with it,—which never could have resulted, had each of them gone to any other,[2]—then, at the moment when the sight from the eyes, and the whiteness from the object which, in contact with the eyes, produces the colour, meet in mid course,[3] the eye becomes filled with sight, and then begins to see, and the result is, not *sight*,[4] but a seeing eye; while the object which, together with the eye, gave birth to the appearance of the colour, is invested with whiteness, and thus here, too, the effect produced is, not whiteness, but *a white* stick or stone or whatever object it may be, the surface of which happens to be coloured with such a colour. And so it is with all other qualities,—we must take the same view of *hard* and *hot* and everything else, viz. that, as we before said, nothing has an absolute existence by itself, but that all effects are produced by a relation and intercourse between patient and agent, and varied in their results according to the kind of movement.[5] For to conceive of both an agent and also a patient in any *one*

D

E

157

distinction between ἀλλοίωσις and *actual* movement, such as that of sight or sound, which he goes on to describe. And after much consideration, I think this is the true meaning of the passage.

1 As sound with ear, smell with nose, etc. The γένεσις of the sense of sight or smell or hearing is quicker than the γένεσις of decay, faded colour, change of bulk, etc., which are the slow and gradual, but not less real, effects of the kind of κίνησις called ἀλλοίωσις.

2 *e. g.* sound to nose, or smell to eye.

3 Or, in a mutual relation to each other (μεταξύ). So inf. p. 182. A, φέρεσθαι ἕκαστον τούτων ἅμα αἰσθήσει μεταξὺ τοῦ ποιοῦντός τε καὶ πάσχοντος.

4 Since ὄψις has no οὐσία of its own.

5 Mere ἀλλοίωσις, or κίνησις ἐν φορᾷ.

thing singly, so as to deny motion,[1] is, they tell us, an impossibility. There can be no agent, till it has come into contact with a patient, nor a patient, unless it has an agent. And that which, by being in contact with one thing, is an agent, becomes in turn a patient combined with some other thing.[2] So that from all these considerations we must conceive, as I said at first, that no one quality can exist singly and by itself; it only *becomes* so-and-so to the particular person who perceives it; and absolute existence must be taken away from everything, even though we, partly from familiarity and partly B from want of skill, have been compelled to use it for many purposes[3] in our late discussion. We ought not, however, as the philosophers tell us, to concede the existence of anything belonging to me or to anybody else; nor 'this' nor 'that,' nor any other term that tends to fix a thing as constant. We should speak of them according to the true nature of the phenomena, as 'brought into being,' or 'created,' or 'perishing,' or 'being altered.' For if one adopts any term that fixes existence, he is easily proved to be in the wrong; we ought to use the above expressions both of things severally and of an aggregate of many,—such generalisations as they C convey by the terms 'man', or 'stone', or any particular creature or kind of things.[4] Well, Theætetus, do these doctrines seem nice? Would you like a further taste of them, as of food that you relish?

Theæt. I don't know, Socrates; indeed, I cannot make up

---

[1] "Non licere, ut aiunt, firme in una re animadvertere."—*Stallbaum.* The exact sense of παγίως is not clear. It appears, from the addition of ὡς φασὶν, to have been some philosophical formula, equivalent to a negation of κίνησις.

[2] Fire in contact with water is a *patient*, being extinguished by it. But in contact with straw it is an *agent*, for it consumes it.

[3] Or simply, 'often'. We have said ἔστι where we should have said γίγνεται, *e. g.* τὰ δὲ γεννώμενα οὕτω δὴ θάττω ἐστὶν, etc.

[4] These are abstractions, ἰδέαι, not individual οὐσίαι They are non-existent to those who do not see them, and are only brought into being as speculations or subjects of conversation. Though Plato was fond of the doctrine, there is clearly irony in his way of putting it here.

my mind even about you, whether you are stating what you really think, or are making an experiment on me.

Soc. Do you forget, my friend, that I myself neither know anything of these matters nor claim them as my own. I am not the parent; I only act as man-midwife to you, and that is why I employ charms and set by you these clever things¹ for you to take a taste of them severally, till at last I help you to   D bring your own views to light. When that has been done, I will then examine whether it shall prove of empty air or a product of real genius. Take heart then, and don't give in, but bravely and like a man answer what you really think about the questions I may put.

Theæt. Ask me then.

XIII. *Soc.* Then tell me once more, whether you accept the doctrine, that nothing really *is*, but *becomes* always right and good, as well as such other qualities as we lately spoke of.²

Theæt. Well, Socrates, now that I hear you arguing in this way, it does seem to me in the highest degree reasonable, and that we should view the matter as you have put it.

Soc. Then don't let us leave off while any part of the argu-   E ment is incomplete. We have yet to discuss the subject of dreams, and of madness among other diseases,³ and such fancies as result from wrong hearing, or wrong seeing, or any other false perception.⁴ For you are aware, of course, that in all such cases as these the argument we maintained⁵ is allowed to

¹ Like φάρμακα ὠκυτόκια, drugs for procuring a speedy delivery. The usual metaphor from serving up viands is here inapplicable; and there seems a little confusion between the φάρμακα and the γενέσθαι τῶν ἀρεσκόντων preceding, unless this also refers to what patients call 'nice physic'.

² As hard and soft, hot and cold. He asks, if the rule holds in morals as well as in physics. Before we can conclude that αἴσθησις is the sole test of existence, we must further inquire if it is always to be trusted And the fallacious nature of it, as in dreams, ghosts, etc., shews that it is not so.

³ Cases of mistaken αἴσθησις, which shews that it is not really ἐπιστήμη, but is liable to error and delusion.

⁴ Lit. 'which it (μανία) is commonly said to hear wrongly', etc.

⁵ That αἴσθησις was ἐπιστήμη.

be proved false, since in these states and conditions there
assuredly *are* such things as 'false perceptions'; and so far 158
from each man's fancies being true for himself, absolutely
nothing of what seems, really is so to him.[1]

Theæt. Nothing can be more true than what you say,
Socrates.

Soc. Then what reply to these facts remains for one who
takes as his axiom that 'Perception is Knowledge', and that
what each man fancies is so to him who fancies it?

Theæt. For my own part, Socrates, I hesitate to say I
have no reply to give, because just now you blamed me for
saying so. For in truth I cannot dispute, that people who are
mad or dreaming do imagine what is false, when some of them   B
fancy they are gods, and others that they have wings, and conceive themselves in their sleep to be flying.

Soc. Here is another difficulty about them, which I think
you will understand, and especially about the question of such
imaginings being mere dreams or sober realities.[2]

Theæt. What is that?

Soc. What I dare say you have often heard people asking,
what *proof* a man can show, if any one should ask him as
at the present moment, whether we are asleep, and dreaming
of all that is now in our thoughts, or awake, and talking to
each other in sober earnest.   C

Theæt. Well, certainly, Socrates, it is hard to say by what
proof we could demonstrate it. For all the details are the
same in both, and go together like counterparts.[3] For instance,

---

[1] For if any single αἴσθησις was right, he would not be mad on that point.
This case differs from the sense of heat or cold, etc., where it may be urged that
it really is hot to one man and cold to another at the same time.

[2] It is not easy to *prove* that things happen merely in fancy, since at the
time the conviction upon you is equally strong. Hence it would be rash to
argue that αἴσθησις is true when you are awake, but false when you are asleep,
and Protagoras may be right in saying that what seems to a man, that is so to
him. As a test of existence, αἴσθησις can be worth little, if it is as often false
as true.

[3] A dream is like a reality, and we sometimes say a reality is like a dream.

in the conversation we have just held, we might, for aught there is to prevent it, fancy we had been talking to each other in a dream; and conversely, when in a dream we fancy we are talking to each other,[1] the latter case is strangely like the former.

Soc. You see then that to raise the doubt is at least not difficult, when it is called in question whether we are really talking or only dreaming.[2] Nay, I go further, and say that if we are half of our lives asleep, and the other half awake, in   D each of these periods our minds are convinced that whatever opinions present themselves to us, these are really and certainly true; so that for the same general duration we say these are realities to us as much as those; and we insist on the truth of both alike.

Theæt. Certainly we do.

Soc. Is not the very same to be said about diseases and mad-fits, except that the *time* is not in this case the same?

Theæt. Rightly remarked.

Soc. What then? Is truth to be determined by the length or shortness of time?

Theæt. That would indeed be absurd in many respects.   E

Soc. Can you then show any other clear proof which of these opinions are true?

Theæt. I don't think I can.

XIV. *Soc.* Then let me tell you the course of reasoning that would be pursued by those who make it an axiom that 'Whatever seems, that *is* so to him who fancies it.'[3] And if I mistake not, their argument is conveyed by a question, as thus:—" If, Theætetus, a thing is *entirely* different, has it any property the same as another thing?" Now mind, we are not to conceive the subject of the question to be *partly* the same as

---

[1] Reading διαλέγεσθαι for διηγεῖσθαι, on which corruption see sup. p 143. B. As διηγεῖσθαι ὀνείρατα can only mean 'to describe dreams,' it is hard to get an intelligible sense out of the vulgate. I think also that ὀνείρατα was interpolated as the object to the corrupt reading διηγεῖσθαι.

[2] Thus it is not always easy to say if an αἴσθησις is true or false.

[3] The school of those who believe only in the evidence of the senses.

and partly different from the other, but as wholly and entirely different.

Theæt. I say then that it is impossible for a thing to have 159 any quality that is the same, either in its property or in any other respect,[1] when it is quite different.

Soc. Must we not then allow that a thing of this sort is also unlike the other?

Theæt. I suppose so.

Soc. Then if it happens that a thing is *getting* like or unlike something, viz. either to itself or to something else, we shall say that while it is thus assimilating itself it is becoming the same, and while it is varying from it, different.[2]

Theæt. That cannot be otherwise.

Soc. And we said before, I think, that the agents in nature were infinite in number, and so also the patients.

Theæt. We did.

Soc. And also that one thing in union with another will produce not the same, but different results from what it would in combination with something else?

Theæt. Assuredly so.   B

Soc. Now then let us speak of myself and yourself and of the agents that affect us, according to the same reasoning, and talk about Socrates in health and Socrates out of health. Are we to say the one case is like or unlike to the other?

Theæt. Do you mean by 'Socrates out of health' Socrates *as a whole*[3] compared with him also as a whole when in health?

Soc. You are quite right in your surmise: that is just what I mean.

Theæt. Then, of course, I say *unlike.*

Soc. Then he is also *another* Socrates, in precisely the same way as he is unlike?[4]

---

[1] Potentially or in appearance.

[2] For if ἕτερον is ἀνόμοιον, then ἀνόμοιον must be ἕτερον.

[3] Not merely in features, or hair, or height, etc., which would be the same, or nearly so, in both states.

[4] If he is ὅλως ἀνόμοιος, he must be ὅλως ἕτερος. Here then is one fallacy

Theæt. We must allow that.

Soc. And you will say the same, of course, of Socrates C asleep, and in any of the states we just before mentioned ?[1]

Theæt. I shall.

Soc. Will not now any one of those things that are in their nature agents, when it gets hold of Socrates in good health, deal with him as one person, and when out of health, as another ?[2]

Theæt. Of course that will be so.

Soc. Then in such case I, as the patient, and it as the agent, will produce between us different results ?

Theæt. Of course.

Soc. Then when I drink wine, being in good health, it seems to me both fragrant and sweet to the taste.

Theæt. Yes.

Soc. We assume that it produced, in accordance with what we have before stated,—that is to say, the agent and the patient together, and in mutual motion and relation with each D other,—both sweetness and a sensation of it. This sensation on the part of the patient[3] made his tongue to be sentient; and the sweetness from the wine, having a motion of its own in respect of the patient,[4] made the wine sweet to the healthy tongue, in reality as well as in appearance.[5]

Theæt. Undoubtedly our former admissions were to this effect.

of αἴσθησις. It makes ὁ αὐτὸς appear ἕτερος under certain circumstances. The argument goes on to discuss another fallacy resulting from different bodily states, that the same wine is, and is not, agreeable to the taste.

[1] μαινόμενον ἢ ὀνειρώττοντα, p. 158. B.

[2] Since ἄλλο ἄλλῳ ξυμμιγνύμενον ἕτερα γεννήσει.

[3] Compare ὄψις πρὸς τῶν ὀφθαλμῶν, sup. p. 156. E. The power or faculty of tasting was exerted on or exercised by the organ of the tongue.

[4] This is not very clear in itself, but he had said ἅμα φερόμενα ἀμφότερα just before, and he is bound to show that the product is the result of κίνησις. As sup. p. 156, there is no οὐσία of any quality; there is only a special γένεσις between two for the time being, and this takes place διὰ τὸ πλησιάζειν. But the γλυκύτης does not come till the wine has met the tongue.

[5] For τὰ δοκοῦντα ἀληθῆ ἐστὶ τῷ δοκοῦντι, p. 158. E.

Soc. But when the wine finds me out of health, in the first place it finds me really and truly not the same person; for it came to me before[1] when I was unlike my present self.

Theæt. Yes

Soc. Then Socrates in this, the unhealthy, condition, and E the drinking of the wine, together produce on the tongue a sense of sourness, and in the wine a sourness which comes into being for him;[2] and they make the wine not indeed sourness, but sour, and me not the sense of it, but sentient.

Theæt. Quite so.

Soc. Then I, under these circumstances, shall always have the same perception,—for the sense of the other[3] is itself different, and makes the person perceiving it different both 160 in character and in identity,—and the thing which acts on me as an agent, if it were in contact with another, would never produce the same results and so become the same. For by producing a different result from a different patient it will itself become of a different character.

Theæt. All that is true.

Soc. And I shall not become sentient of this or that for myself, nor will it be of this particular quality for itself.[4]

Theæt. Certainly not.

Soc. But of course I must become sentient of something, when I become sentient at all,—for one can't become sentient and yet sentient of nothing, you know,—and the agent must become something to somebody, when it becomes sweet or sour B or anything of that kind. For to become sweet, yet sweet to nobody, is an impossibility.

Theæt. Assuredly.

---

[1] Or simply, 'it comes to me', the aorists being used in the general or *gnomic* sense.

[2] The words καὶ φερομένην seem to me to have been interpolated from ἡ γλυκύτης περὶ αὐτὸν φερομένη above.

[3] ι. e. ὑγιαίνοντος.

[4] ι. e I am a sentient *to the wine*, and the wine is sour *to me*,—there must be a patient if there is an agent, and the converse. See Lucret. 1. 440.

Soc. There is nothing left for it then but that this 'being' or 'becoming' must be mutual; for, as we said, the being of both is necessarily coupled together. But it is not coupled to any other than what we are,[1] nor to ourselves, it remains therefore for us only to be coupled to each other.[2] So that, whether one uses the term 'is', he must say it is to somebody, or it is of something, or in relation to something, or the term 'becomes'; but he must not himself speak of anything either C 'being' or 'becoming' singly of itself, nor allow another to use such expressions. This is the conclusion which the foregoing argument indicates.

Theæt. It certainly does so, Socrates.

Soc. Then when anything which affects me is an agent to me and not to another, I also have perception of it, but another has not.

Theæt. Of course.

Soc. It follows that my sense is a true sense to me; for it belongs to a union of which I am an essential member. Thus I am a judge, as Protagoras affirms, of whatever is, and I can fairly say that it is so to me; or of what is not, that it is not.

Theæt. It seems so.

XV. *Soc* I want to know then how, if I am infallible D and cannot be mistaken in my own views about what is or becomes, I can fail to have an accurate knowledge in whatever I have perception.

Theæt. That would be impossible.

Soc. Then you put it very well when you said that Knowledge is nothing else than Perception. So it comes to the same thing whether, according to Homer and Heraclitus and all that school, all things are ever in motion, like currents, or, according to Protagoras, that wisest of men, man is the measure of all things; or, according to *Theætetus*, these facts being assumed, E

---

[1] Since the result would be different.

[2] If there must be a σύνδεσις, and there cannot be a coupling of self to self, nor of wine to wine, it must be of wine to self.

that Perception comes to be Knowledge.[1]   Is it not so, Theætetus?   Must we say this doctrine is a newly-born brat of
yours, and that I have been concerned only in the delivery
of it?   Or how say you?

Theæt.   So it must be, Socrates.

Soc.   This child of ours then, as it seems,—whatever it be
worth,—we have at last brought into the world.   And now
that it has been born, the next step will be to perform the
ceremony (in good earnest, too,) of going round by reasoning 161
on it, taking good heed that the thing born does not turn out
unworthy of being brought up,[2]—a mere creature of air and
a sham.   Or do *you* think that, as the doctrine is your's, we are
bound to rear and not to discard it?   Or will you patiently
see it put to the test of inquiry, and not be very full of wrath
if some one should try to take it from you, like a first child
from a mother?

Theod.   Theætetus will stand it, Socrates; he is not ill-
natured   But tell me, in Heaven's name, is it not, on the
other hand, just the other way?[3]

Soc.   You are quite an enthusiast in argument, and a
worthy good man, Theodore, if you think I am a sort of
bag of words, and can easily take out of it and deliver a speech
to prove that all this is again *not* so!   You don't comprehend
what comes of these discussions,[4] that none of these arguments   B

---

[1] From all these statements the inference is deduced that there is no stable
οὐσία in anything.   There is great wit in a passage that ironically puts Theætetus on a level with Protagoras, Heraclitus, and Homer,—to say nothing of the
bathos in placing him last.

[2] It may perhaps be inferred from this passage, that the question whether
an infant should be reared or discarded and exposed was generally discussed and
decided at the carrying of the child round the family hearth on the fifth day
after birth.   The metaphor is here applied to the careful examination of an
object to see if there is a weak point anywhere, *e. g.* in a fortification.

[3] Theodore knows Socrates' skill in proving black is white and white is
black.   He rightly suspects that after pretending to accept, he is going to
disprove the doctrine of Protagoras

[4] He playfully uses τὸ γιγνόμενον in place of τὸ ὄν.

proceeds from me,[1] but always from the party who converses with me, and that I myself know nothing more, except just this trifling matter, how to get a subject from some other clever person, and to give it a fairly good reception.[2] And so I will endeavour now to get this from our young friend here, and not to say it myself.

Theod. What you propose, Socrates, is better, and therefore act accordingly.

XVI. *Soc.* Do you know, then, Theodore, what it is that I am surprised at in your companion Protagoras?

Theæt. What is that?

C

Soc. The general account of his views he has given charmingly,—how that what seems to each man *is* so to him. But I wonder at the beginning of his treatise, and that he did not commence his 'Essay on Truth' with these words, 'The measure of all things is a Pig'—or a baboon, or some other still more outlandish specimen of such creatures as are endowed with the faculty for feeling.[3] For then he would have began his address to us in grand style, and indeed with no little contempt for us, by showing that while we have been looking up to him, as to a god, for his wisdom, he all the time was no better in respect of intelligence than the tadpole of a frog,[4] not to say, than any other human being.[5] For if that is to be true and real to each man, which he forms an opinion of through perception, and if one man is not to give a decision on the state and the condition of another any better than himself, nor to have any better right to form a judgment about the opinion of another, as to its truth or falsehood, but if (I repeat)

D

---

[1] Whom you call a θύλακος.

[2] As a nurse takes a child from its parent.

[3] Since λόγος, reason, the attribute of ἄνθρωπος, has no place in mere perception, αἴσθησις.

[4] γυρῖνος seems a noun, formed like κορακῖνος, from γυρὸς, describing the rounded form of a tadpole.

[5] Protagoras' doctrine, that αἴσθησις is the sole test of what is, was obviously destructive of his own claim to superior wisdom. The irony here is admirable.

each man is to have his own views peculiar to himself,[1] and
in all these cases they are right and true views,—then why
in the world, my friend, is Protagoras so very wise as justly
to be thought worthy of being the teacher of others with large   E
fees,[2] while *we* are less intelligent, and have to go to school to
him, when every man is in fact the measure of his own
wisdom? Surely we must say that Protagoras is talking
mere clap-trap in all this! As for my own poor services, and
my obstetric art, I say nothing about the ridicule that we incur,
and indeed, the whole profession and business of dialectic.
For of course our examination of and our attempt to refute
each other's fancies and opinions, if every man's are equally   162
right, must be a long and dreary waste of breath, if Protagoras'
'Truth' is true, and did not give its oracular utterances from
the depths of the book in mere joke.

Theod. Socrates, the man is a friend of mine, as you yourself just now said. Therefore I don't wish to have Protagoras
proved to be in the wrong through any admissions of mine,
nor on the other hand to insist that my views are right against
your convictions. Do therefore once more take Theætetus, who
certainly seemed just now to respond very readily to your
appeal.

Soc. Supposing, Theodore, you were to go to Sparta, to
visit the wrestling-schools; would you expect to look at others   B
stripped, some of them but poor figures, without having to
display against theirs your own form by taking off your clothes
to compare it?[3]

Theod. Do you think I would not, if I thought they were
likely to allow me, and to comply with my request? Just so
I hope now to persuade you to let me remain a mere spectator,

---

[1] *e g* the opinion that the weather is hot, though another may say it
is cold

[2] Perhaps the μετὰ should be omitted, and we should construe ἀξιοῦσθαι
μεγάλων μισθῶν.

[3] Do you expect to be present at our conversation without a single question
being put to yourself?

and not to drag me to the wrestling-ground, old and stiff as
I am, but to try a throw with one who is younger and more
pliant in limb.

XVII. *Soc.* Well, Theodore, if that is what pleases you,
it does not displease me, as they say in the proverb. Once   C
more then we must go to our clever friend[1] Theætetus. Come,
now, Theætetus, to take first the views we have discussed,—
do you not share in our surprise that you will thereby prove
all at once not inferior in wisdom to any man, or even any
god? For you don't suppose that Protagoras' 'Measure' is
said at all less in reference to gods than to men?

Theæt. Indeed I don't. And, to reply to your question,
I am very much surprised; for when we were discussing in
what way they meant to say 'That which seems to each man,   D
is so to him,' it seemed to me very well said; but now it has
suddenly turned out quite otherwise.[2]

Soc. Ah! you are young, my friend, and therefore your
ears and your mind are readily open to[3] the lecture you have
heard. (But don't be alarmed); for in reply to this, Protagoras,
or some one in his behalf, will say, 'My fine fellows, men and
boys, here you are sitting together and talking fine, and bringing forward the gods, though I expressly exempt them both in
speaking and in my writings, and decline to say whether there   E
are or are not such beings.[4] You only say what the mass of
mankind would accept if they heard it,—that it is strange
if human beings, each and severally, shall have no superiority
in respect of wisdom over any animal; but as for proof or
cogent argument, you adduce none whatever; you adopt a

---

[1] An ironical allusion to his doctrine of αἴσθησις, which makes one man as
wise as another.

[2] In μεταπίπτειν there is a metaphor from dice, or the throwing up of
a piece of pot, ὄστρακον. Theætetus, in his youthful piety, revolts against
a doctrine that makes the gods no wiser than men.

[3] ὑπακούεις more literally is 'you respond to,' *i. e.* you are caught by the
popular address,—the shallow clap-trap you have heard.

[4] See Cic. *De Nat. Deor.* i. § 63.

view that is a mere probability, albeit, if Theodore or any
other geometer chose to employ it, he would be worth simply
nothing.   Consider therefore, both you and Theodore, if you
are prepared to accept statements made on such weighty 163
matters by mere probabilities and plausible talk

Theæt. Why, Socrates, neither you nor we should say that
was right.

Soc. Then we must view the matter in a different light, as
it appears from what you and Theodore say.

Theæt. Differently, by all means.

Soc. Then let us proceed thus to the inquiry, whether, in
truth, Knowledge and Perception are the same or something
different.   For it was to this that the whole of our argument
was directed, and for this that we mooted all those strange
outlandish theories, was it not?

Theæt. It was, without doubt

Soc. Shall we then allow, that when we perceive things   B
by the faculties of seeing or hearing, we at the same time also
know *every* particular about them?[1]   For instance, if we have
not learned the dialect of foreigners, are we to say that we
don't hear them, when they speak, or that we don't hear them
with understanding?   So again, if we don't know letters,
when we look at them are we to say that we don't see them,
or to insist that, of course, if we see them, we understand
them?

Theæt. Only just this part of them, Socrates, that we
actually see and hear, we shall say we understand; that is
to say, that we both see and know the shape and colour of the
letters, and hear and apprehend the shrill or the deep tones of   C
the voices; but such explanations of the meaning of both as
writing-masters or interpreters give, we shall allow that we do
not know, as we do not realise them by seeing or hearing.

Soc. Bravo, Theætetus!   To encourage you, I shall not
care to raise any objection to your answer.

---

[1] Another proof that ἐπιστήμη is not mere αἴσθησις consists in the fact that
the latter may be partial, *i. e.* fall short of full intelligence.

XVIII. But see, there is another difficulty coming upon us; and it is for you to consider how we can get clear of it.[1]

Theæt. What is that?

Soc A question of this kind, which might be put —'Is it possible, if a man once became acquainted with something, that while he yet has a recollection of it and retains it, he should not *know* the very fact that he remembers?' But perhaps I am using more words than I need; I merely wish to ask, if a man who has learnt something does not know it when he remembers it?

Theæt. How can that be, Socrates? What you say would be a miracle.

Soc. Perhaps the fault is mine for talking nonsense. But consider: you call seeing perceiving, do you not, and sight perception?

Theæt. I do.

Soc. It follows then that a man who has seen something has 'become acquainted' with what he saw, according to our late axiom ?[2]

Theæt. Yes.

Soc Well! I suppose you allow there is such a faculty as Memory?

Theæt. Yes.

Soc. Is it of nothing or of something?

Theæt. Of something, of course.

Soc. Therefore of something or other that one learnt and had a perception of ?

Theæt. Of course.

Soc. Well, now, if a man saw an object, I suppose he remembers it sometimes?

---

[1] Another difficulty in the doctrine that αἴσθησις is ἐπιστήμη, consists in the fact, that the knowledge gained by αἴσθησις may be lasting and real, though the αἴσθησις no longer exists. In this case memory has succeeded to perception. But if the two things are different in some respect, then the one cannot be the other

[2] That ἐπιστήμη was αἴσθησις.

Theæt. He does.

Soc. When he shuts his eyes? Or does he forget it when he does that?

Theæt. Why, it would be rather bold to assert that!

Soc. But we must assert it, if we are to maintain our 164 axiom as before. Otherwise, it is gone.[1]

Theæt. Upon my word, I suspect as much; but I have not a sufficiently clear apprehension. Say therefore how.

Soc. Why, in this way: he who sees, we say, has become acquainted with that which he saw; for sight and sense and knowledge are allowed to be all one.

Theæt. Undoubtedly.

Soc. Well, but one who by sight became acquainted with what he saw, if he shuts his eyes remembers it[2] and yet does not see it. Is it not so?

Theæt. Yes.

Soc. But this 'does'nt see it' means 'does'nt know it', if,   B as we say, 'he sees' means 'he knows'.

Theæt. True.

Soc. It follows then, that, if a man became acquainted with something, though he still remembers it, he does not know it, since he does not actually see it! But we said that would be a miracle, if it really happened.

Theæt. What you say is very true.

Soc. It seems then that something which is impossible *does* occur, if one maintains that Knowledge and Perception are identical.

Theæt. It seems so.

Soc. Then we must assert that each of these is distinct.

Theæt. So it appears.

Soc. What then can Knowledge be? We must discuss it   C

---

[1] Because there would not be ἐπιστήμη if there were not αἴσθησις. The common, but solecistic, reading εἰ σώσοιμεν still holds its place in the texts. We must read εἰ σώσομεν.

[2] Since μνήμη was just before allowed to be a necessary consequence of ἐπιστήμη.

again, as it seems, from the beginning. Yet what are you
going to do, Theætetus?

Theæt. About what?

Soc. Like some dunghill cock, we seem to me to have
suddenly left the argument and to crow before we gained the
victory.[1]

Theæt. How can that be?

Soc. It appears to me that we are acting like mere con-
troversialists; we form our premises with regard to the common
acceptation of words,[2] and we are content by such means to get
the better in the argument. Thus, while we profess to be
philosophers and not mere wranglers, we are unconsciously
doing the very same as those learned and skillful disputants.[3]   D

Theæt. At present I don't see your meaning.

Soc. Well, then, I will try to make what I mean to say
clear to you on this subject.[4] We asked, you know, if a man
who has learnt something, and has it in mind, can be said not
to know it. And by taking the case of one who has seen an
object, and afterwards, with his eyes shut, *remembers* it though
he does not see it, we said that he did not know it[5] and yet had
it in memory, which was impossible. And so this fine story
of Protagoras'[6] came to an end, and with it your's, of the
identity of Knowledge and Perception.

Theæt. It seems so.   E

Soc. But it would not, I suspect, my friend, had the
author of that other saying[7] been alive, but he would have

---

[1] To be exulting and boasting before we are sure of victory. The metaphor
is ἀποπηδᾶν is taken from cock-fighting. The contrary is ἐπιπηδᾶν, Ar. *Vesp.*
705.

[2] Whereas αἴσθησις is capable of a meaning more recondite than the common
one of 'sensation'. So, too, as he shows below, 'Knowledge' may have a
sense in which a man may be said 'tó know and not to know'.

[3] The *eristic* school, of whom Plato speaks with evident irony.

[4] περὶ αὐτῶν refers to ταὐτὰ just above.

[5] If αἴσθησις was ἐπιστήμη.

[6] The μέτρον ἕκαστος, amounting virtually to the same as the other saw,
'sense is knowledge'

[7] There is a little subtle irony in μῦθος, as distinct from λόγος.

brought effective aid to it. At present, we are abusing it when it has none to befriend it. Indeed, it seems that even the guardians whom Protagoras left behind him,—our friend Theodore here is one,—don't care to interfere in its behalf. Well, then, we will make the venture ourselves, and come to its aid for the sake of fair play.[1]

Theod. Nay, Socrates, it is Callias, the son of Hipponicus, who is the guardian, rather than I. Somehow or other, *we* 165 took to geometry, and got away from the science of bare words. However, we shall feel obliged to you, if you undertake the defence of him.[2]

Soc. Very good: then observe, Theodore, the kind of aid *I* am going to bring.[3] For a man might have to make admissions still more damaging than those we have just made, if he did not carefully attend to the lax use of phrases,—how we are in the habit of saying 'yes' and 'no' in our ordinary answers.[4] Must I tell *you* how that is, or Theætetus?

Theod. Rather tell us all in common, only let the younger be the respondent; for if he gets a throw he will be in a less awkward plight[5]

XIX. *Soc.* I tell you then what is the most formidable B question of all. It is to this effect: Can a man at once know something, and yet *not* know what he knows?

Theod. What answer now[6] are we to give, Theætetus?

---

[1] If others will not do for the sake of their deceased friend

[2] Or 'of it', the λόγος Theodore means, that though for a time he was in the school of Protagoras, he can hardly be regarded as a representative of his doctrines.

[3] Viz. which consists in showing yet further difficulties in accepting his doctrine, (or what is equivalent to it, αἴσθησις is ἐπιστήμη.)

[4] *i. e.* we ought to use them with more reservation, or in a more qualified sense

[5] An old man falling, or thrown in wrestling, is more likely to excite sympathy. So Euripides says of the aged Hecuba, that if she does not submit, but is dragged away as a captive, ἀσχημονήσει ἐκ νέου βραχίονος σπασθεῖσα. (*Hec.* 407.) To the same metaphor belongs ἀφύκτῳ below. Compare πάλαισμ' ἄφυκτον, Æsch. *Eum.* 746.

[6] Theodore has been warned not to say 'yes' and 'no' too rashly.

Theæt. That it is impossible, in *my* opinion.

Soc. Not at all,—if you intend to maintain that seeing is knowing. For how will you deal with a question that cannot be evaded,—caught, as the saying is, in a tank,[1]—when some undaunted man asks, as he covers one of your eyes with his hand, ' Whether you see his mantle with that covered one ?'

C

Theæt. I suppose I shall say that I don't with that, but I do with the other.

Soc. Then you at once see and don't see the same object ?[2]

Theæt Under those circumstances—yes.

Soc. I don't put that reservation[3] (he will reply), nor did I ask you about the *how*; but simply whether, what you know, you also don't know. It now appears that you see what you don't see ; and you have already allowed that seeing is knowing and not seeing is not knowing. Consider then what results from these premises.

Theæt. Well, I see on reflection that it is just the contrary of what I said before.[4]

D

Soc. And perhaps, my estimable friend, more difficulties of the same kind would have occured to you, if any one put further questions to you ; ' Can a man have a keen or a dull knowledge ?[5] Can he *know* close by, but not far off ? Can he *know* the same thing loudly and gently ?' There are countless questions of the like kind, by asking which in the course of his argument a light-armed fighting-man serving for hire[6] might

---

[1] See below, p 174, A. Pits cut in the limestone rock, and not very deep, were probably called φρέατα when there was some spring, and λάκκοι when they were only tanks for catching rain-water.

[2] A palpable sophism, and only given in jest, or to puzzle a young man. For the shutting of one eye does not exclude sight ; and sight *quoquo modo* is αἴσθησις.

[3] Lit. ' I don't order you to give that (restricted) answer.'

[4] Viz that it was impossible at once to know and not to know.

[5] Will epithets appropriate to sight (physically) be also appropriate to mental apprehension ? He adds an example from *sound*.

[6] A Sophist. The metaphor is drawn, and cleverly sustained, from captives taken by troops in ambuscade.

entrap you, when you had defined Knowledge to be the same
as Perception. Then, making a direct assault on seeing and
smelling and senses of that sort,[1] he would show your definition
to be wrong, pressing you hard and allowing you no rest,   E
till at last, in your admiration of that much-to-be-coveted
wisdom of his, you had allowed yourself to be bound hand and
foot by him; and then,[2] having got you fairly in his power,
and tied you to a string of other captives, he would at last
consent to ransom you for whatever sum you could agree on
between you. What defence then, you may perhaps ask,
would Protagoras make in aid of his own doctrine? Must we
essay to state it?

Theæt. By all means.

XX. *Soc.* Well, then, he will say all that *we* say in his
behalf, and more than that, will make a direct attack on us,
expressing his contempt for us in these terms:—' So then this 166
worthy, this Socrates, because a mere lad, when asked by him
if it were possible for one and the same man at once to
remember and yet not to know the same thing, was timid,
and in his timidity said 'no', through having no faculty of
foresight,[3]—has held up my illustrious self to ridicule in his
reasonings! Whereas, in fact, you most heedless of disputants,[4]
Socrates, the case stands thus: when you are examining any
views of mine, and to this end propose a question about them,
if the party questioned gives such a reply as I should give,
and is beaten, then *I* am proved to be in the wrong; but if his
answer is of a different sort, then the person himself to whom   B
it was put. For instance,—do you imagine anyone will
concede to you that, if the memory abides in anyone of something that he underwent, it is a feeling of the same kind as it
was when he underwent it,[5] viz. now that he no longer feels

---

[1] See p. 156, B.

[2] For οὗ δή, lit. ' whereupon', we should perhaps read μέχρι οὗ δή.

[3] *i. e.* that an affirmative answer might prove right in the end.

[4] He is supposed to speak like one a little vexed

[5] A man knows the feeling of having some operation performed, because he

it? Or again, do you suppose he will hesitate to admit that thus it *is* possible for the same man to know and not to know the same thing? Or, should he fear such an admission as that, do you suppose he will allow you to maintain that a person who is undergoing some change[1] is identical with what he was before he began to undergo it? In other words, that a man is *the* particular person always, and not several, and that by a process of *becoming* this or that in endless variety, if a *becoming* unlike should take place in him?—for I suppose we must be careful not to catch up each other's words.[2] No! my very fine fellow, he will say, do come to the precise point of my assertion, and prove it wrong if you can. Show that our perceptions are *not* special and peculiar to each of us, or that, if they are such, not at all the more for that what *seems* to anyone *becomes* so to him, and to him only (or say, '*is* so to him', if we may use the verb 'to be') to whom it seems.[3] But in talking of swine and baboons, you not only act swinishly yourself, but you persuade your hearers to do the same towards my writings; which is not fair play. For I insist that the truth is as I have stated in my book; that each of us is a measure of what is and what is not; though I allow that there is an enormous difference between one man and another in this very respect, that to one man this seems to be and therefore

C

D

once experienced it; and he knows it also, because he retains a vivid recollection of it Yet the knowledge derived from μνήμη is not the same as the knowledge derived from πάθος. In this sense he may be truly enough said "to know and not to know."

[1] Lit 'who is getting unlike' his former self, *e. g.* getting thin, or fat, or grey-haired, etc. The argument is, that it is as possible 'to know and yet not to know,' as 'to be the same and yet not the same.' So we familiarly say to a friend, 'Why, you are quite another man !'

[2] *i. e.* to speak quite correctly, and use γίγνεσθαι and not εἶναι.

[3] Show that I am wrong in saying, that if I feel it hot, and you feel it cold, it *is* hot to me and it *is* cold to you, and that there really is no other true test of hot or cold but our respective feelings. For I maintain that this is a true doctrine, etc.

E

is, to another that.[1] In this sense I am far from denying that
there is such a thing as wisdom or a wise man. On the
contrary, I even affirm that this very man *is* wise, who, by
producing a change in another, to whom certain things seem
and are bad, makes them seem and be good.[2] Now don't carp
at my statement again, from the way in which I have expressed   E
it, but take this illustration that you may know my meaning
still more clearly. Recal to mind what we said before, that
if a man is out of health, what he takes both seems and is
nauseous to him, albeit it seems and is just the contrary to
one in health. Now, it is not for us to make either of these[3]
wiser on the subject, for indeed that is not possible; nor are   167
we to find fault with him, and assure him that the sick man
is a stupid fellow for thinking so-and-so, but the healthy man
is wise for thinking something quite different. No ! we must
change him so as to take the other view; for this other
disposition is a better one Just so in educating him, we must
alter him from the bad mental habit to the better; only, while
your physician effects this by drugs, your professor does it
by argument. For we cannot say that a person had *false*
opinions once, but somebody made him hold *the truth* afterwards; he cannot think what to him is not, nor anything
else than what he feels; but this must always be true to him.
In fact, the case is this: when through a vitious condition   B
of mind, men hold vitious opinions, a right condition causes
them to hold right opinions These views[4] some people through
want of practice in reasoning call 'true views'; all *I* say is,

---

[1] One man may have more sensible and reasonable views than another, and
thus σοφία may exist in a relative, though it cannot in an absolute sense. One
man may think that all law is tyranny, another, that it is the preservation of
society. The former is a perverse view, but to the man who holds it, it *is*
tyranny. You cannot argue him out of it; alter the man's sentiments by education, and his convictions will alter themselves.

[2] Justice, temperance, liberality, etc.

[3] Either the man ᾧ φαίνεται κακὰ or ᾧ φαίνεται πικρὰ, etc

[4] The words τὰ φαντάσματα are perhaps interpolated.

that the one sort of views is *better* than the other sort, but
not at all *truer*. And, my dear Socrates, I am very far from
calling wise men frogs.[1] As far as they deal with men's
bodies, I call them physicians; as far as with plants, husband-
men.[2] For I affirm that even these, if any of their plants are
out of health, produce in them good and healthy sensations,   C
and such as are true to it,[3] instead of vitious ones; just as
your wise and good speakers cause that what is good instead
of what is bad should appear to states to be right. For I lay
it down as an axiom, that ‘Whatever each state considers just
and right, that is so to it, so long as it holds them to be so.’[4]
Only your wise man makes what is good to seem and therefore
to be good, instead of what is bad being true to them[5] in any
particular case. In the same way your professor also, if he
can train his pupils after this method, is wise, and deserves   D
large sums of money from those instructed by him. According
to this view, then, some persons are wiser than others, and
yet no one holds false views. No! whether you like it or not,
you must submit to be ‘a measure’. For by considerations
of the above kind[6] the statement we are discussing is shown
to be consistent. If you can call it in question by denying
its premises, do so by arguing against it in a discourse, or,

¹ As having no other criterion than αἴσθησις, which they have in common
with the humblest animal.

² This is a curious remark, and seems to refer to the ψυχή which the ancients
thought all animate and organic beings possessed. Scientifically, it is true that
a plant can have illness as well as an animal, and that such illness may or may
not be curable by treatment. But the αἴσθησις of a plant is only its suscepti-
bility, or perhaps, its irritability. We do not know that it has *feeling* in the
sense in which we are endowed with it

³ Since τὰ δοκοῦντα are ἀληθῆ τῷ δοκοῦντι.

⁴ This is the νόμιμον δίκαιον of Aristotle The difficulty of assuming any
one code or course of action to be exclusively moral, is very great. Polygamy
is illegal in one country and legal in another, the same may be said of stealing,
kidnapping, lying, or even homicide.

⁵ By ὄντων αὐτοῖς he means, ἃ φαίνεται καὶ ἔστιν αὐτοῖς, i. e. αληθῆ ἐστίν.

⁶ Viz. by admitting *degrees* of goodness,—relative goodness, though there is
no absolute good.

if you prefer that method, by questions: for even this[1] is not
to be shunned by a man of sense. Act, however, in this way;
don't be *unfair* in your questions; for it is most unreasonable   E
that one who professes to care about uprightness and truth
should do nothing but cheat all through his discourse. And
I call it cheating, in circumstances like the present, when
a man does not observe the just distinction between arguing
and conversing,[2]—in the former saying what he does not really
mean, and trying to throw his adversary by every means in his
power, in the latter[3] speaking always in earnest and setting
up the other on his legs again, by pointing out to him only
those failures and slips in which he had been led into error
by himself or by a course of bad teaching before[4] For if you 168
act thus towards them, those who converse with you will
blame themselves for their own confusion and perplexity, and
not you[5]; rather, they will run after you and love you, and
dislike themselves. They will find a refuge from their own
ignorance in philosophy, in order that they may become what
they were not, and be rid of their former selves. If, however,
you take the contrary course, as most do, then the contrary
will be the result: you will make those who associate with
you to hate learning instead of loving it, when they get old.   B
So, if you will take my advice, as I said before, you will
not dispute in a surly and captious spirit,[6] but bring yourself

---

[1] The Sophists generally preferred the continuous method, as being more
suited to their ἐπιδείξεις. See Sophist. p. 217. D.

[2] A sketch of the method of the eristic school,—the ἀντιλογικοὶ, who cared
for nothing but victory in the argument, and so took advantage of every quibble
and cavil.

[3] The word διαλέγεσθαι is perhaps interpolated.

[4] Not taking advantage of any hasty statement, but generously letting him
retract it, and only pressing him hard where his own obstinacy or perversity, or
the false instructions of sophists, have misled him.

[5] They will see that their discomfiture is really due to erroneous views, and
not to the sharpness or quibbling of the adversary. Plato is evidently con-
trasting the method followed by Socrates with that adopted by the Sophists.

[6] Or, 'as if fighting with an enemy.'

down to our level with sentiments of kindness, and consider
in good earnest what we mean when we lay it down as a plain
truth that 'all things are in motion,' and that 'whatever
seems to each, that is so to a state or to an individual alike.'
From a right view of these doctrines you will further consider
whether Knowledge and Perception are the same or different,
and not, as you did just now, from the familiar use of phrases
and words,[1] which the many drag and distort to bear any sense   C
they please, and so cause each other every kind of perplexity.
Such, Theodorus, is the aid I have rendered[2] by way of taking
your friend's part, to the best of my poor abilities,—a small
contribution from a small store. Had he been himself alive,
he would have defended his own views in more effective
language.[3]

XXI. *Theod.* You are joking, Socrates: you *have* come to
the good man's aid with real spirit and courage.

Soc. I am glad you think so, my friend. And now tell
me; did you notice Protagoras' saying just now, with reproach to us, that by holding our conversation with a boy we
made use of a boy's natural timidity to argue against his   D
doctrines; and how, scolding us for what he called our
pleasantry, and magnifying his own doctrine of "Measure",
he bade us be serious in dealing with his argument?

Theod. Of course I noticed that, Socrates.

Soc. Well then, do you advise us to do as he tells us?

Theod. I do, by all means.

Soc. Do you observe then that all the present company
except yourself are mere boys? If therefore we are to comply
with our friend's wishes, you and I, by questioning and
answering each other, must give our serious attention to his   E
argument, that he may not have this to complain of in us, that

---

[1] That is, by taking such terms as αἴσθησις and εἰδέναι in too narrow, and
the merely popular sense

[2] The reading is doubtful. Perhaps προσήρκεσα μὲν instead of προσηρξάμην.

[3] The literal sense may be intended to convey some irony, 'with more pretentiousness.'

we have for the second time discussed the matter in joke by addressing ourselves to striplings.

Theod. Well, is not Theætetus likely to follow an argument through all its mazes better than many who wear long beards?

Soc. Yes, but not better than you, Theodore. So don't suppose that it is my duty to take the part of your friend, now that he is no more, by every means in my power, while you 169 are not bound to help him at all. Come, my friend, go with just me so far,—'tis but a little way,—till we ascertain whether *you* have a special claim to be an authority about diagrams, or all are as competent as you, for their own purposes, in astronomy and those other sciences in which, you know, you are considered to excel [1]

Theod. It is not easy, Socrates, when one sits by you, to avoid giving one's views on any subject. I am afraid my joke was little to the purpose, when I said you would excuse me from stripping to show myself, as they do at Lacedæmon. No, *you* seem rather to incline to the practice of Sciron [2] At Lacedæmon they tell you either to strip or to go; but you B seem rather to act like Antaeus,[3] for when anyone meets you in company you don't let him go till you have made him strip and compelled him to try a throw with you in the argument.

Soc. You have admirably, Theodore, expressed my weakness by your simile. I, however, am stouter than those you speak of; for 'ere now many and many a Hercules and a Theseus, on meeting me,—men strong in talk,[4]—have pounded me right well; but I don't give it up for all that, so strong a desire has taken possession of my soul for exercises of this C kind Do not therefore on your part refuse to anoint yourself for a bout with me, and so to benefit both yourself and me.[5]

---

[1] *Wrongly*, if the doctrine μέτρον ἕκαστος is true.

[2] A bandit who made strangers strip their mantles and give them up to him.

[3] The giant of Libya who compelled strangers to wrestle with him. The meaning is, that Socrates allows no alternative.

[4] The Sophists.

[5] He speaks of gymnastic exercises as recommended by ἰατρική

Theod. I have not another word to say against it, so take any course you please Come of it what may, I must endure the fate, whatever it may be, of which you have woven the thread, and submit to be questioned on these subjects,—not, however, further than the limits you propose[1] shall I allow myself to be examined by you.

Soc. Well, even so far will do. And I pray you, be very careful about this,—don't let us inadvertently make our discussion after the puerile fashion,[2] lest some one should again reproach us with it.

Theod. Be quite sure I shall make every effort in my power.

XXII. *Soc.* Let us then in the first instance once more get a grip of the same difficulty as before; let us see whether we rightly or wrongly took offence at and found fault with the statement, because it made every man to be wise enough in himself; and whether Protagoras was right or wrong in granting that, in respect of better or worse,[3] some people were superior to others; and that such really were wise. Was it not so ?

Theod. It was.

Soc. Well, now, if he had been here in person to make that admission, instead of our making it for him as supporters of his cause, there would have been no need to take up the subject again and try to get it settled in this way. As it is, perhaps some one may say that we have no authority[4] to make the admission on his behalf, and therefore it is the more proper course to come to an agreement between ourselves[5] on this very question; for it makes a material difference in the argument whether it is as Protagoras says, or the other way

D

E

---

[1] See p. 169. init.

[2] Don't let us incur the taunt of Protagoras, since we two are men, and not mere boys.

[3] Though not in *truth* and *falsehood* See p. 166. D.

[4] As οὐ σοφούς

[5] Making it rather a matter of conviction for ourselves than of admission on his part, which it may be we have no right to make.

Theod. What you say is quite true.

Soc. Then let us arrive at this agreement as briefly as possible, and from no other premises than those supplied by his own reasoning. 170

Theod. How?

Soc. In this way. He says, I think, that 'what *seems* to each man, that *is* so to him who thinks it so'?

Theod. He does say that.

Soc. Then, Protagoras, we also on our parts state the view of a human being,[1] or rather, the views of all human beings, when we affirm that everybody in the world thinks himself wiser than others in some things, and others wiser than himself in other things; nay more, that when people are in danger in military service or in times of pestilence or in a storm at sea, they behave towards those who hold the command in any such cases as they would towards divine powers, expecting to be saved by them, though in fact their only superiority over others consists in their knowledge. In fact, human life is full of such instances; men seek others to teach and to direct both themselves and their domestic animals and even their trades; or they think themselves competent to teach and competent to direct. Now, in all these cases what are we to say, but that the men themselves believe that wisdom or want of information resides with themselves? B

Theod. That is the only conclusion we can come to.

Soc. They think, then, that wisdom means a true view, and ignorance means a false opinion.

Theod. Of course. C

Soc. Then how, Protagoras, are we to deal with your proposition? Must we say that these men *always* think truly, or sometimes truly and sometimes falsely? For, if they do

[1] Who is a μέτρον, and therefore whose opinion is true to *him*. He goes on to show, that as most people think Protagoras is wrong, therefore to them he *is* wrong in saying that all men are equally wise. Common experience, he argues, shows that men do believe in different degrees of wisdom both in themselves and in others.

both, it follows of course that they do not always think the truth, but sometimes truth and sometimes falsehood. For consider, Theodore, whether anyone is likely, either of Protagoras' party or yourself, to contend, that no man thinks another man is ignorant and holds false views?

Theod. Why, that is incredible, Socrates.

Soc. And yet that is the strait into which the argument is brought, that affirms man to be the measure of all things.[1]   D

Theod. How is that?

Soc. When you, after making up your own mind on some point, express to me your own opinion upon it; granted that this opinion, according to his statement, is true to *you*; yet may not we, the rest of the world, become judges of your judgment, or do we conclude that your views are invariably right? Is it not rather the case, that multitudes set their opinion in opposition to your's, believing that your judgment and your opinion are alike wrong?

Theod. Yes, by heaven, Socrates, a mighty host indeed, as   E Homer says, who are ever causing me a world of trouble.

Soc. What then? Shall we say, that in such cases you hold opinions that are true to you, but are false to the vast majority?

Theod. That inference seems inevitable, if we are to follow the argument.

Soc. And what must Protagoras himself infer? Surely he must grant either that neither he nor the majority really believe (as we know they do not) man is a measure,—in which case the truth he has written about is truth to no one at all; or that *he* thinks so, but the majority do not; and then you are aware 171 that, in the first place, the more there are who don't think so, compared with those who do, in the same degree it *is* truth more than it is not truth.

---

[1] If practically men admit they may be wrong, or ignorant, and therefore that Protagoras may be wrong, his proposition falls by his own *dictum*. it is true to them that what Protagoras says is not true.

Theod. That must be so, if the opinion of each is to to be the test of truth.[1]

Soc. In the second place, his doctrine brings us to this sublime conclusion: in allowing that all hold opinions that are real to them, he of course concedes that the views of those who hold the contrary to his, and by which they consider his views are false, are true to them.

Theod. Undoubtedly.

Soc. Then he would be granting that his own opinion was   B untrue, in allowing that their's is true, who think him in the wrong.

Theod. It certainly is so.

Soc. But the others, I presume, do not allow that they are mistaken.

Theod. Indeed, they do not.

Soc And he allows that such a conviction in them also[2] is true,—to judge from what he has written.

Theod. Then by all without exception, and by Protagoras himself among the first,[3] this 'truth' of his is called in question, —or rather let us say, by him at all events it will be conceded, when he allows that the person who speaks against his, Protagoras', views, hold a true opinion,—then, I say, Protagoras himself must admit, that neither a dog nor your ordinary man   C is a measure of anything about which he is uninformed[4]   Is it not so?

Theod. It is.

Soc. Since then his doctrine is called in question by all,

---

[1] Protagoras' doctrine is self-refuting: his own test of truth shows that his opinions are not true, for the great majority are against him   A remark of the most profound significance, if applied to the thought and the profession of our own age   Very few persons indeed get beyond the assumption, which they mistake for the conviction, that they are in the right.

[2] ι e as well as his own convictions.

[3] Since he is the enunciator of a self-destructive dogma.

[4] In allowing that his adversaries may be right, Protagoras allows that only the intelligent are μέτρα, in as much as they are on a par with himself.

Protagoras' Truth will be true to nobody,—neither to himself nor to anyone else.

Theod. We are running down my friend too hardly, Socrates.

Soc. Nay, my good sir, I am not quite sure that we are not outrunning the truth.   Certainly, it must be presumed that he, being older, is wiser than we.   Suppose now he were   D at this very moment to raise his head and shoulders up from the floor,[1] he would very likely scold us roundly, me for talking nonsense and you for assenting to it, and then suddenly disappear and be off before we could stop him.   As that cannot be, however, I suppose we must make use of ourselves as measures, to find out what we are, and to say always what we think.   Thus, we may surely now affirm that anyone will allow this,—that one man is wiser, or is less well-informed, than another.

Theod. I think we may.

XXIII. *Soc.* Shall we also say that the argument will stand best by the guiding-line we drew[2] when we were advocating Protagoras' doctrine,—viz. that things *generally* are as they   E seem to be to each person,—hot, or dry, or sweet, or of any other quality of the like kind; but that, if anywhere and in any instances he shall grant that one man is superior to another, he must be content to say, that not any woman or boy or even any creature is competent to undertake its own cure, by its knowledge of what is wholesome for it, but that here, if anywhere, one *is* superior to another.

Theod. That is my opinion.

Soc. Then in politics also he must admit that in respect of 172 what is honourable and dishonourable, just and unjust, lawful or not lawful, whatever code of morality a city lays down for itself, believing it to be right, these things are so to it in

---

[1] Like a ghost from the ἀναπίεσμα of a theatre, or a spirit conjured up by necromancy

[2] A metaphor from school-masters under-ruling boys' copy-books

rcality.[1]   In these matters one citizen is not wiser than
another, nor one state than another state.   But in enacting
laws that are for or against its own interest, he will allow that
the opinion of one state, or of one adviser of the state, is
superior in respect of truth to that of another; for he will
hardly venture to affirm, that whatever laws a state may have   B
enacted with the full belief that they are to its own advantage,
they will also in the end prove to be such.[2]   But in the case of
which I am speaking,—in matters of justice or injustice, lawful
and unlawful, men are prepared to insist that none of these has
an inherent quality of its own by nature[3]; they will not allow
more, than that what has been accepted by the state in common
becomes true so soon as it shall have been so accepted, and
so long as it may remain on the statutes.   And even those who
do not accept Protagoras' doctrine of ' measure', take the above
view of wisdom [4]—But argument after argument seems coming
upon us, Theodore, and a greater after a less.   C

Theod.   Well, Socrates, we have leisure for it, I suppose.

Soc.   It seems so.   Indeed, I have often, my good sir,
observed on other occasions not less than now, how very
naturally those who have spent much time in philosophic
inquiries, when they come into law-courts appear ridiculous as
orators.[5]

    [1] *e g.* if a state enacts that polygamy is lawful, it becomes νόμιμον δίκαιον,
and no one will be entitled to say that for that state the practice is wrong.   It
is not easy to gainsay this proposition, since the law of the state is the standard
and criterion of men's actions rather than the moral law, respecting which there
is no universal agreement

    [2] *e g.* Protection, or free-trade, may be political theories tried in good faith,
but found to be failures.   In predicting results, some ἐπιστήμη far superior to
mere αἴσθησις is required.

    [3] That there is no φύσει δίκαιον, but only νόμῳ δίκαιον, (see Arist. *Eth. Nic.*
V. 10), *i.e.* no αὐτὸ τὸ δίκαιον possessing a δικαιοσύνη of its own.

    [4] Viz. to the denial of any objective or absolute and invariable truth, but
admitting that one man may be wiser than another as a ξύμβουλος, etc.

    [5] A man who has studied δίκαιον is often no match for the τὸ πιθανὸν of the
pleaders.   This sentiment, several times repeated by Plato, probably has reference to the condemnation of Socrates; and if so, it was never spoken by Socrates

Theod. In what sense do you say this?

Soc. It appears to me that those who have been conversant from their youth with law-courts and assemblies of that kind, compared with those who have been educated in philosophy and kindred pursuits, have been brought up like slaves com-   D
pared with free men.

Theod. In what respect?

Soc. In so far as the latter, just as you remarked, always have leisure, and hold their conversations at their own convenience and in peace. As we are now taking up one subject after another for the third time, so do your philosophers, if the new theme should please them better than the one proposed, as it has done in our case. Nor does it now concern them at all whether they speak in brief or at length, if they do but get hold of the truth. Whereas your lawyers always speak under pressure of time,—for the water as it keeps running does not allow them to loiter,—and it is not in their power to make their   E
addresses on any subject they may please, for the counsel on the other side stands there exercising a constraint over them in the shape of a brief which he reads as they speak,[1] and beyond the limits of which they must not digress. His speeches are always about one who is as much a slave as himself,[2] and are addressed to one seated there as lord and master, who holds justice in his hand[3]; nor do the pleadings ever digress into any other topic, but are confined always strictly to the legal question, albeit it is often a race for dear life.[4] So that from all these causes your lawyers become   173

at all. This event rankled in the mind of Plato and embittered his existence. He never forgot and he never forgave the Athenians for it. But it is not genuine Socratic language or sentiment.

[1] The clause added in the MSS., ἣν ἀντωμοσίαν καλοῦσιν, 'is probably an interpolation, as Stallbaum also thinks, following Abresch.

[2] *i.e* the plaintiff or the defendant.

[3] The judge or the presiding archon is compared to a τύραννος, παρ' ἑαυτῷ τὸ δίκαιον ἔχων, Æsch. *Prom.* 194

[4] "Ne tum quidem quum ipsa vita defendenda est, aliquid dicere liceat, quod ad ipsam causam non pertinere videatur."—*Stallbaum.*

shrewd and sharp, well knowing how to flatter their master in word as well as how to gratify him in act,[1] yet small and warped in their minds; for their growth in goodness, with their straightforwardness and freedom of character, has been taken from them by their having been slaves from their boyhood, which has constrained them to be always engaged in some crooked business or other, by burdening their yet tender minds with heavy loads of dangers and fears.[2] Now, as they cannot bear such a load supported by justice and truth, they turn in quite early life to falsehood and to wronging each other, and thus in many respects become warped and stunted, and so turn out men from mere striplings[3] without any sound principles in their minds, and very clever and wise they have become,—in their own opinions. So much then for the lawyers, Theodore; and now for those of our set,[4]—do you propose that we should describe them fully, or dismiss them for the present and resume our former subject, that we may not, as we said just now,[5] make too free a use of our independence and our privilege of taking up one topic in place of another?

Theod. Not so, Socrates, on any account; let us rather discuss their character in full. For, as you very well observed, it is not that we, the acting party on these occasions, are the slaves of our subjects, but rather our subjects are, as it were, domestics, and each of them awaits our convenience for being brought to a conclusion, whenever it may seem good to us. For we have not in our company either any juryman, or,

B

C

---

[1] Viz. by bribes.

[2] They *dare* not prefer justice to chicanery, lest they should lose influence, popularity, or profit. Plato's animosity against the lawyers is here curiously shown. He is full of bitter thoughts about the condemnation of his great master.

[3] The *youth* of the advocates, συνήγοροι, is several times alluded to by Aristophanes, *e. g.* Ach. 685, *Vesp* 687—91. The metaphor is from plants of crooked growth; 'si te alio pravum detorseris,' Hor. *Sat.* ιι. 2, 55.

[4] The philosophers.

[5] Οὔκουν σχολὴν ἄγομεν, p. 172. C.

as the poets have, any spectator, standing by us to find fault or
to call us to order.

XXIV. *Soc.* Let us proceed then to our description, as it
seems we must, and as such is your pleasure, taking the best
specimens of the class[1], for why should one mention such
as spend their time in philosophy to little or no purpose?
Well, then, your best men, I suppose, in the first place do
not so ·much as know their way into the agora at all, nor
the site of any law-court or of the council-hall, or any other   D
meeting-place in the city; and as for laws and decrees of the
people, they neither see them written nor hear them read.
Much less do they know of the secret intrigues of political
parties for securing to themselves[2] state-offices, and treasonable
meetings and dinners,[3] and serenades with your *danseuses*,
—they don't even dream of doing such things. Then whether
any citizen is well-born or ill-born, or what harm attaches to
anyone by hereditary descent,[4] either from the male or the
female line, they know no more than (as the proverb is,) how
many quarts there are of sea-water. Nay, he does'nt even
know that he does'nt know all this; for 'tis not to be supposed   E
that he keeps out of the way of such things for the sake of
credit, but in real truth his body alone is there in the city and
' in town', while his mind and thoughts, regarding all such
concernments as trifling and mere nothings, despise them and
soar all abroad, ' measuring,' as Pindar says, ' the regions below
the earth and those upon it, star-gazing in heaven's heights,'
and investigating fully the true nature of the phenomena of 174

---

[1] Having called the school of philosophers a χορὸs, he keeps up the metaphor
in κορυφαῖοι, the leading men, οἱ ἄκροι. The οἱ φαῦλοι are perhaps the Sophists;
or Plato may glance at some school which he disliked, as that of Antisthenes.

[2] We should read ἐπ' ἀρχαῖς, as Ar *Lysist.* 577, τοὺς πιλοῦντας ἐπ' ἀρχαῖς.

[3] Ar *Vesp.* 495, οὗτος ὀψωνεῖν ἔοιχ' ἄνθρωπος ἐπὶ τυραννίδι. The guileless
and simple character of Socrates is hyperbolically described. Compare *Phædr*
p. 230, C, D

[4] Those called ἐναγεῖς, who were thought to be under some ancestral curse
See *Phædr.* p 244 E

each and every part of the universe,[1] never bringing themselves down to the level of any of the objects that are near.

Theod. In what sense do you say this, Socrates?

Soc. Just as Thales, Theodore, when he was star-gazing and had his eyes on the sky, contrived to tumble into a pit, and so incurred the ridicule of a smart and pretty Thracian slave-girl, for being so eager to know what was in heaven above him, while he failed to notice what lay before him at his very feet,—so the same banter holds good against all who devote their time to philosophy. It is simply true that persons of that profession know nothing about other people, even their own neighbours,—not only as to their occupations, but almost whether they are human beings at all, or some other kind of creature. No! what *man* is, and what better objects and destinies such a nature has than the lower animals,—that is what he not only inquires, but takes pains thoroughly to understand. You see what I mean, Theodore, don't you? **B**

Theod. I do; what you say is quite true.

Soc. And the consequence is, my friend, that your philosopher both in his private dealings and intercourse, and in his public appearance on any occasion,—when he is obliged to talk either in a law-court or elsewhere about matters before his feet and in his sight, makes himself ridiculous, not merely to Thracian slave-girls, but to the people generally, by tumbling into pits and into every sort of puzzle through want of practice; and his awkwardness is something terrible to see, and suggests the notion that he must be a downright fool For in the attacks on people's characters he has nothing personal to say against any one, as knowing no harm of anybody from the want of practice;[2] and thus from being at a loss he appears **C** **D**

---

[1] In his earlier career, and probably at the time when Aristophanes satirized him in the *Nubes* for that course of teaching, Socrates had given his attention to physical science, as he himself avows in the *Phædo*, p. 96. He appears to have been instructed at first by Archelaus in the doctrines of Anaxagoras.

[2] A severe satire on the *profession* of a backslider, who has 'got up' all the gossip against his neighbours.

ridiculous. So, too, in the praises and high-flown eulogies of
others, by letting people see that he laughs not affectedly but
in all sincerity, he is regarded as a silly giggler. For when he
hears an encomium on a tyrant or a king, he imagines that he
hears one of your stock-keepers,—a swineherd, for instance, or
a shepherd, or a neat-herd—called happy for draining a great
deal of milk[1]; only he thinks that kings feed and suck an
animal more discontented and more fond of laying plots than
the herdsmen do. He thinks, moreover, that such a potentate
must of necessity be quite as churlish and uninformed as the
herdsmen are, from his want of leisure, seated as he is in his
castle on a hill like a shepherd in the midst of his fold.[2] / And   E
when he is told that some one who owns ten thousand or more
plethra of land[3] possesses an astonishing quantity, he imagines
that what he hears is but a very small amount, accustomed as
he is to look at the whole world. / And when they speak in
praise of men's pedigrees, and tell you that so-and-so is of high
birth because he can show seven rich ancestors, he regards
such a commendation as coming from people who see dimly
and only a few years back, and who from defect of education 175
cannot have their eyes always on the universe,[4] nor consider
that every individual has had countless myriads of ancestors,
in which rich and poor, kings and slaves, foreign and Greek
have been born into the world in millions for every one, be he
who he may ; but when men pride themselves on a list of five-
and twenty forefathers, and carry back a pedigree to Hercules
the son of Amphitryon, it does seem to him surprising that they
should make these trumpery reckonings; and he laughs at

---

[1] The word βδάλλειν, allied to βδέλλα, 'a leech,' was applied to the habit of
herdsmen draining the milk by sucking the cow's or goat's udder, a charge
sometimes brought against the innocent hedgehog. The allusion is to the taxes
drawn by the tyrant from his subjects.

[2] Lit. 'Having his fortress built round him like a sheep-fold on a mountain.'
The very name τύραννος seems connected with τύρσις, *Tor*, in reference to the
acropolis on which his castle is built.

[3] A *plethrum* contained 10,000 square feet.

[4] Or 'on general principles', perhaps.

them for not being able to see that the twenty-fifth from
Amphitryon still further back was just what fortune happened   B
to make him, and so to get rid of the conceit of a senseless
mind.   In all such cases then as the above, a character of this
kind is ridiculed by the many, partly for being proud, as he is
thought, partly for not knowing the most obvious facts and
being at a loss on every occasion.

Theod. You describe, Socrates, exactly what happens in
the world.

XXV.   *Soc.* But when, my friend, *he*, the philosopher,
has drawn some of these men of law above the level of their
courts,—in other words, when some one has consented at his   C
request to exceed the narrow limits of ' What harm do I do to
you, or you to me?' and to rise to the contemplation of justice
and injustice in its true nature,[1]—what each of them is, and
how they differ from each other and from everything else,—
and to leave such questions as ' Whether a king is happy
because he owns much gold', for inquiries about the nature of
sovereignty, and of human happiness and misery in general,—
what these two things really are, and in what way it is the duty
of one who is by birth human to attain the one and to escape
the other,—when it comes to the turn of that small-minded
but shrewd man of law to give his views on all these subjects,
then he plays the counterpart of the philosopher in the courts;
he is giddy from being suspended aloft,[2] and looking upwards
from his height he loses heart from being so unused to it.
Then he gets perplexed, and by his unintelligible talk he   D
makes himself laughed at, not indeed by Thracian slave-girls,
nor by anyone else who is uneducated,—for they are not
intelligent enough,—but by all who have had an education
of the contrary kind to slaves.[3]   Such, Theodore, is the

[1] From the special or particular to the general and the abstract.

[2] In the regions of the higher speculation. The words allude to πάλιν
ἐλκύσῃ *sup.* Some such language may have suggested to Aristophanes to
exhibit Socrates in his aerial κρεμάθρα in the *Nubes.*

[3] ἀνδραπόδοις, while it more obviously refers to Θρᾴτταις, is meant to include
the δικανικοὶ, whom he had just before called ' slaves.'

character of each; the one, that of a person brought up in
reality with the ideas of a gentleman and with leisure at his
disposal,—the philosopher, in fact, as you call him,—who may   E
be excused for seeming a simpleton and a mere nobody when
he is suddenly required to do the services of a slave,—for
instance, if he does not know how to pack a portmanteau or
to flavour a relishing dish, or words of flattery.[1] The other
is the character of one who knows how to perform all these
services[2] thoroughly and promptly when called upon, but does
not know how to throw his mantle over his right shoulder like
a freeborn gentleman, much less has acquired the fitting language for rightly praising the true life of the gods and of
happy men.[3]   176

Theod. Ah! Socrates, if you could persuade all men to
think so, as you do me, there would be more peace and less
evils in this world of ours.

Soc. But it is impossible, Theodore, either that evils
should be abolished,—for there must ever be some principle
antagonistic to good,[4]—or that they should take up their abode
among the gods. No! they must range this mortal nature and
this world of ours, and there is no help for it. And this is
just the reason why we should try to flee away from this to
the other life with all possible speed. Now by this flight   B

---

[1] As in the Gorgias, where he calls rhetoric μαγειρική, Plato refers to the
ῥήτορες and δικανικοὶ under the disguised name of 'slaves.' The general sense
is, that a philosopher need not know how to cook, but a cook (*i. e.* a politician)
ought to know something about justice The meaning is cleverly disguised, the
point being to disparage the lawyers as an illiberal uneducated set, slaves in
mind if not in social position. See *Vesp.* 1132, *Aves* 1568.

[2] Those of flattery and nicely seasoned conversation.

[2] The δικανικὸς, with all his ready talk and cunning, has never realised
that true μουσική which enables the philosopher to praise the god-like life as it
deserves.

[4] This is, perhaps, the best account that ever has been or ever can be given
of the existence of evil on earth Good and evil stand in the same necessary
correlation as heat and cold, dryness and moisture, hardness and softness,
i. e. we cannot conceive of the one apart from the other.

I mean the making oneself as like to God as is possible for
man; and this likeness consists in becoming just and holy
with the highest intelligence.[1] But alas! my friend, 'tis by
no means easy to persuade people that, after all, it is not for
the sake of that, for which most men tell us we ought to shun
vice and to pursue virtue, that we are bound to practice the
one and not the other,—that is, merely that one may be
thought not bad, or to be positively good,—for all this is what
they call old wives' gossip, as it seems to me. No! let us
state the truth thus:—God is in no way and in none of his   c
dealings unjust; on the contrary, he is as just as it is possible
to conceive, and there is nothing so like to him, as any one
of us who on his own part has learnt to be as just as he can
be.   On this point turns the question whether a man is really
clever, or good for nothing and a man only in name. Yes!
it is the knowledge of this which is wisdom and true virtue,
while ignorance of it shows a want of instruction and a
baseness than cannot be mistaken. All the other kinds of
cleverness and wisdom, as they are commonly thought to be,
in places of political influence are simply vulgar,[2] and in the
arts are tradesman-like. If, therefore, any of these men act   D
unjustly, or say or do what is unholy, far the best course to
take with them is not to allow that they can be clever by
wrong-doing[3].   For as it is, they glory in their shame, and
they flatter themselves they are being told they are no fools,

---

[1] The Platonic φρόνησις is the highest condition of perfection and happiness
in this world and the next.

[2] The οἱ δυνατοὶ, e g. ῥήτορες and δημαγωγοὶ, without true ideas of justice,
are merely playing the parts of slaves in a comedy.

[3] This shows how far Socrates was before modern society in the love of truth
and the bold rebuking of pretentiousness. We should not expect now-a-days,
if a man were boasting of his cleverness in some questionable transaction on the
stock-exchange, to hear another say to him in public, "Sir, you were not clever,
you were simply a rogue" It would be difficult to show that Plato knew the
writings of his contemporary Thucydides, but there is a passage remarkably
like this in Thuc. iii. 82, § 15, ῥᾷον δ' οἱ πολλοὶ κακοῦργοι ὄντες δεξιοὶ κέκληνται,
ἢ ἀμαθεῖς ἀγαθοί· καὶ τῷ μὲν αἰσχύνονται, ἐπὶ δὲ τῷ ἀγάλλονται.

no mere encumbrances of earth, but *men*, such as those should
be who have any hope of coming off safely in the turmoil of
politics. We should therefore tell them the plain truth; that
they are what they think they are not,[1] all the more because
they think they are not. For they do not know the penalty
of injustice, which of all things they ought least to be ignorant
of. It is not what they suppose, stripes or capital punishment,
nothing of which in many cases has to be borne by the unrighteous; no! it is a penalty from which there is no escape.   E

Theod. Of what then do you speak?

Soc. My dear friend, there are two examples set before us
in the order of things; that of the godlike, which is most
blessed, that of the godless, which is most miserable. Now
those who from stupidity and utter want of intelligence do not
see that this is so, are unconscious that they get more and 177
more like the one through their unrighteous acts, and more
and more unlike the other. And the penalty of this ignorance
they pay by living the life, the example of which they are
bringing themselves to resemble.[2] And if we tell them, that
if they don't cease from that cleverness of theirs, in the other
life they will never find entrance into that blessed abode that
is free from all evil,[3] but will pass a grovelling existence in
this lower world, like to their present sojourn upon it, bad
in company with bad,—if we tell them this, they will more
than ever regard themselves as clever fellows, who are up to
anything, being lectured by a parcel of fools.

Theod. That is true indeed, Socrates.

Soc. Indeed it is. There is one result, however, from   B

---

[1] *i e* λῆροι and γῆς ἄλλως ἄχθη.

[2] Viz. τὸν ἄθλιον. See *Phaedr.* p. 248. D.

[3] In this remarkable and magnificent passage we must not suppose that
Plato's view is precisely the same as our materialistic notions of 'heaven',
though it is very probable that the speculations in the well-known passage
of the *Phaedo*, p 110, very much influenced men's opinions, as now generally
held on the subject. The Orphic doctrine of the succession of life both here and
in a future state (Pind. *Ol.* ii 57, etc) is the point principally here alluded to.

which they cannot escape: if they hold a private conversation,
giving and hearing reasons on the course of life they so disparage, and consent like men to stand their ground without
running like cowards for some considerable time, then, my
good sir, they get strangely out of temper with themselves
at the end of the argument, and all that fine eloquence of
theirs fades away, so that they seem no better than boys.
However, on these subjects, as the discussion of them at
present is out of place, let us say no more, or our first argument will be overwhelmed by the flood of ideas that will pour   C
in upon us.   Let us then, if you please, return to our former
inquiries.

   Theod. I confess that to me, Socrates, these extra subjects
are fully as pleasant to hear about: for they are easier for one
of my age to follow up. However, as you wish it, let us go
back again to our former subject.

   XXVI. *Soc.* Well, then, I think we were about that
point of the argument where we affirmed that those who take
for their axiom that Being is but Movement,[1] and that ' what
seems to each is so to him to whom it seems', are ready to
insist, that in things in general, and especially in questions of   D
justice, whatever views a city may have adopted as such, as
the expression of her opinion on the subject, to her they *are*
just, so long as they are in force. But when the question
turns on what is her real interest, we maintained that no man
was presumptuous enough in this case to venture on the assertion, that what a state has enacted believing it to be beneficial
to itself, that also is so for as long a time as the enactment
remains; unless, indeed, we are talking about what is beneficial
in name only; which, of course, would be a mere satire on the
subject of our conversation.

   Theod. It would indeed.

   Soc. Then don't let him talk of the mere name, but the   E

---

[1] Like φερομένη γένεσις in *Sophist.* p 246. C., and like οἱ ῥέοντες, οἱ στασιῶται, for the advocates of flux and stability, this is a short formula for expressing
that there is no other οὐσία but that from motion.

reality of that which, under the name of 'beneficial,' is the subject of our inquiry.

Theod. Certainly not.

Soc. Then whatever she means by the name, that, of course, she aims at in her legislation, and all the laws, to the best of her belief and her power, she enacts with a view to her own interest especially. Is there any other end she has in view in making laws?

Theod. Assuredly not.   178

Soc. Does then a state always succeed in this aim, or does every government make occasional mistakes?

Theod. I think that it is often mistaken.

Soc. Perhaps from the following consideration any one might be yet more likely to form the same conclusion; I mean, if he were to put the question respecting the entire class of things which includes *the useful*: that, of course, is one that in its very nature extends also to the future.[1] For, whenever we legislate, we enact our laws with the hope and belief that they will be beneficial for times yet to come, that is, to speak correctly, 'for the future'.

Theod. Of course.

Soc. Come then, let us ask Protagoras, or some of those who maintain his opinions, this question:—'You say, gentlemen, that man is the measure of all things,—of white, heavy, light, all qualities and conditions of that kind whatsoever.   B For, as he has in himself the criterion of them, whatever he feels, believing it to be such, is so to him, and constitutes a true belief. Now, is this not so?'

Theod. It is so.

Soc. But has he also in himself, Protagoras, (we shall say,)

---

[1] By *synthesis*, the whole class of things or results which are prospective should be taken into consideration, since this will include τὸ ὠφέλιμον, as not referring only to present time. The argument is, that the doctrine of μέτρον cannot possibly apply to anything except present feeling; *e.g.* in legislation, medical treatment, preparing food, farming, etc., there must be a knowledge which will foresee effects.

a criterion of what will be ?   Do things happen exactly as one
thinks they will happen, when one has formed a certain opinion   C
about them ?   For instance, in the feeling of heat, when some
person ignorant of medicine has conceived the idea that a fever
will seize him, and there will be in him a certain feverishness,
but another, a physician, forms a contrary opinion, according to
the opinion of which are we to say that the result will be ?
Or will it be according to both opinions,—will the patient not
feel hot and feverish to the physician, but feel both to himself?

Theod.   That would be absurd, indeed.

Soc.   Yet, I suppose, on the sweetness or sourness that is
yet to be in wine, the opinion of the cultivator alone, and not   D
that of the harp-player, is of authority.

Theod.   Of course.

Soc.   Nor, again, would a trainer in boys' exercises be
likely to judge better than a musician whether a piece of
music when played will be in good or bad tune, though afterwards, when it *is* played, the trainer may háve ear enough to
think it is correct.

Theod.   Certainly not.

Soc.   Well, the judgment of one to whom a dinner is to be
given,—he being no adept at cookery—while the banquet is in
preparation, will be of less weight than that of the cook
respecting the pleasure that is in store for him.   For observe,
we are not at present to insist in our argument on the pleasure   E
that each one now feels, or has felt, but simply on the question,
whether, in what will seem and therefore be pleasant to each,
every man is the best judge for himself.   Would you, Protagoras, be a better judge before-hand than any of the un-
learned of what would be likely to carry conviction to each of
us if you went into court ?[1]

Theod.   Why, Socrates, that is just the point in which
Protagoras specially professed that he himself surpassed all
others.

---

[1] It may be suggested that the word ἰὼν has dropped out after δικαστήριον,
from the similarity of the terminations.

Soc. Of course, my good sir, he did. If he had not, no
one would have conversed with him on payment of a large 179
fee,—I mean, if he had *not* tried to persuade[1] his pupils that
no seer, and indeed nobody else in the world, was likely to
judge better not only what was, but what would seem and
be convincing, than each man for himself.

Theod. Most true.

Soc. Then both legislations and their utility are concerned
with the future; and all will readily grant that of necessity
a state must, in enacting laws often fail in securing its highest
and truest interests.

Theod. Certainly.

Soc. Then we shall give a fair reply to your master, if we
tell him he is bound to allow that one man *is* wiser than   B
another; and that, although such a person is a measure of
truth, yet I, who have no such knowledge, am in no way
bound to become a measure;—a conclusion very different from[2]
that of the argument lately undertaken in his behalf, which
insisted that I was a measure, whether I wished it or not.

Theod It seems to me, Socrates, that the proposition is
best refuted by that consideration (though, indeed, it is also
refuted by this[3]), viz. that it makes the opinions of others to be
of authority, and those opinions have been shown to regard
his statements as altogether untrue.   C

[1] The editors alter μὴ into δὴ or πῃ. I think that what Protagoras told his
pupils was this. "Gentlemen, no one can possibly decide better than your-
selves," *i. e* every man is his own μέτρον. This pleased their vanity, and they
paid him for learning the doctrine   There is a subtle irony in stating the case
thus, when it really was *against* Protagoras' own claims to superior intelligence.

[2] The context seems to require οὐχ ὡς ἄρτι με ἠνάγκαζεν, etc.   The οὐχ is
wanting in the copies

[3] Theodore, after a little pause to think, prefers, as a refutation of Protagoras' statement of μέτρον ἕκαστος, the deduction that, if every man is right,
the majority must be right in thinking him wrong   But he allows the last
argument, that one man *must* be cleverer than another in judging of future
results, to be also a good refutation   Stallbaum, who construes καὶ ταύτῃ ᾖ,
etc , takes ἐκείνη to refer to the argument from utility. Socrates goes on to say
that even more than two ways of refuting such a doctrine might be found.

Soc. There are many others ways, Theodore, in which such a proposition as this might be refuted, that 'every opinion of every man must be true.' But it is more difficult to prove that, in such feelings as each one has at the time, which are the sources of our impressions and of the opinions founded on them, such opinions are not true.[1] Perhaps, indeed, it is not enough to say this: they may even be, and perhaps are, irrefragable; and those who affirm that they are plain and clear, and therefore sure grounds of knowledge, may possibly assert what is really the case. And thus our friend Theætetus is not far from the mark in saying that Perception and Know-ledge are the same thing. We must therefore look at our   D work of art a little closer, as the argument in defence of Protagoras told us to do, and we must examine this doctrine of 'Being is only motion' by ringing it to hear if it sounds cracked or whole. At all events, no small contest about it has arisen, and that with a numerous school.

XXVII. *Theod.* Small! I should say not. Why, in Ionia[2] it is even gaining ground rapidly. The fact is, the followers of Heraclitus support this doctrine very heartily.

Soc. And therefore, friend Theodore, the more carefully we must look into it, and from the very beginning, according to the line they themselves take.   E

Theod. By all means. For indeed, Socrates, *apropos* of these Heracliteans, or as you say, these followers of Homer or others yet earlier[3]—one can no more converse with the disciples themselves of the school of Ephesus, who profess to be well up in the doctrines, than one could with maniacs. For, just like their own teachings, they are ever in motion; and as for staying on one subject or question, or quietly reply-ing or putting a question in their turn, this is no more in them

---

[1] If a man says 'I feel cold', you cannot fairly prove that he is not.

[2] The Ephesian or Heraclitean school.

[3] Orpheus or Musaeus, both of whom some considered contemporaries with, others predecessors of Homer.

than anything; or rather, what is not even a naught[1] is greater 180
compared with the utter absence of rest in these men. No!
if you ask any of them anything, they drag forth as if from
a quiver certain ambiguous wordlets and shoot them off; and
if you try to get some account of this, and to know what it
really means, you will be hit by another term used in a new-
fangled sense, and so will never come to any conclusion in
conversing with any of them. Indeed, they do not themselves
do any better with each other, but they very carefully observe
their own law of never letting anything stable[2] remain either B
in the argument or in their own minds, thinking, I suppose,
that 'stable' is 'stationary'; and with that, you know, they
are openly at war, and even, as far as they can, try to get rid
of it altogether.

Soc. Perhaps, Theodore, you have only seen these men
disputing, and have never had an interview with them in their
moments of peace; for they are no friends of yours. That
kind of language, I suppose, they use to such disciples of theirs
as they wish to make like themselves, when they have a little
more leisure.

Theod. Disciples, indeed, my good sir! Why, with philosophers of that kind no one is a disciple of another. They C
spring up like mushrooms,[3] from whatever source any of them
may chance to have drawn his inspirations; and each one
believes that the other knows nothing. From these men, then,
as I was going on to say, you will never get any explanation if
they can avoid giving it, or even by a stroke of luck. You
must take the men themselves and consider them as a problem.[4]

---

[1] A *minus-naught*, if such a phrase could be used.

[2] As advocates of the doctrine of motion, they keep shifting their own ground
in the argument, being afraid of nothing so much as of the opposite doctrine of
στάσιμον, 'the stationary.' A witty satire on the unsound arguments of the
school in question, and their weakness in dialectic.

[3] αὐτόματοι. The metaphor may be from the Σπαρτοί, or 'sown men,' *i. e.*
sown from the dragon's teeth.

[4] Viz. as the best illustration of their own theory of flux.

Soc. Indeed, you speak quite reasonably. But have we not received this very problem in two ways and from two sources? —from the ancients, who used poetry to conceal their real   D meaning from the multitude, and who taught that the creation of all things,—expressed by 'Ocean' and 'Tethys',—is perpetual motion, and that nothing stands; and from the later philosophers, who, as being more advanced, openly explained their doctrines to all, in order that the very cobblers may understand their wise sayings when they hear them, and may leave off stupidly thinking that some things stand and other things move,[1] and, on being told that *everything* moves, may hold them in due honour.—But I had almost forgot that there are others who openly maintain the very contrary doctrine to these; as for example, that the so-called universe is unmove-   E able[2]; and other propositions which are affirmed by more than one Melissus or Parmenides, in opposition to all these of the Ionian school. Such are, 'that the universe is one,' and that it is 'self-contained and stands still,' because 'it has no place to move in.' Now, my friend, how are we to deal with all these conflicting doctrines? For in our gradual advance, we have fallen between the two without knowing it,[3] and if we don't defeat them and get clear off, we shall be punished as boys are in the wrestling-schools when they play at the game of the 181 line,[4] when they are seized by both sides and dragged to the

---

[1] Which is, at least, the common-sense doctrine. This passage also contains a severe satire on the school of Heraclitus, which Plato, for some unknown reason, appears especially to have disliked. He ridicules the conceit which induced them to give up the *economy* or reserve with which the older men, the poets, taught the doctrine of flux, and to declare openly to all that πάντα κινεῖται.

[2] For τῷ πάντ᾽ ὄνομ᾽ εἶναι compare *Sophist.* p. 242. D, τῶν πάντων καλουμένων.

[3] A metaphor from an army that comes between ambuscades on each side of a narrow gorge

[4] In which the moment one person sets his foot on a line drawn, he was seized by both parties and tugged off like a captive to one side or the other. Probably the side to which he belonged tried to retain him, and the other side

camp of the enemy. It appears to me, therefore, that we ought to examine first the other side, against whom we first made a movement, the 'fluent' school. And, if we should think there is something in what they say, we will join them in dragging our own selves to their side, in our efforts to get away from the others: or if, on the other hand, the party who make the universe stand still[1] should seem to speak more truly, we will run off to them and leave these people who would B move even the immoveable. And again, should we be of opinion that neither side has anything reasonable to say, we shall be ridiculous in supposing that we second-rate inquirers talk sense, and in expressing disapprobation of very old and very learned men. Consider then, Theodore, if it is worth our while to advance in the face of such a danger.[2]

Theod. I should rather say, Socrates, it is not to be endured that we should not fully consider what each of the contending parties have to say.

XXVIII. *Soc.* Consider then we must, as you show such zeal in the cause. It seems to me that our discussion about universal motion should begin with the inquiry, What do they C mean in saying that 'all things move'? What I intend to express may be put thus: Do they affirm that there is one kind of motion, or, as I rather think, that there are two? However, don't let this be my opinion alone, but do you share in it, that we may suffer in common,[3] if it must be. And now tell me: Do you call it *motion* when something changes from one place to another, or even when it turns as on its own axis?[4]

Theod. I do.

again to take him prisoner. The meaning here is, that between the ῥέοντες and the στασιῶται, (the advocates of flux and the advocates of stability,) there is a chance of being carried off to one or the other side. We shall be thought half-and-half men, and so be claimed by them both.

[1] Parmenides and his school.

[2] Viz. that of being γελοῖοι The metaphor from the ambuscade is kept up in προϊέναι.

[3] *i. e.* the discredit of a defeat.

[4] This is *visible* motion, forming a class of its own.

Soc. Let this then be taken for one kind. But when there is no local movement, but a thing is growing old, or becoming D black from being white, or hard from soft, or undergoing any alteration of that kind, are we not justified in describing this as another kind of motion?

Theod. I think so.

Soc. Nay, you cannot avoid it. I reckon therefore two kinds of movement: alteration, and motion in space.

Theod. And rightly.

Soc. Then, after making this distinction, let us proceed to argue with those who say that everything has motion; and let us put to them this question: Do you mean that every thing moves in both ways, that is, both by motion and by alteration, or that some things have both kinds of motion, some only one? E

Theod. Well, really, I don't know what to reply. I suppose they would say, in both ways.

Soc. Why, if they do not, my friend, they will find that˙ things both move and stand still, and the answer that ‘all things are in motion’ will be just as incorrect as that ‘they stand still’.

Theod. That is very true.

Soc. Then, since they must be in motion, and non-motion cannot exist in any of them, it follows that all things move always with all the kinds˙of movement.

182

Theod. It cannot be otherwise.

Soc. Now then mark well this conclusion of theirs. We said, I think, that they explain the origin of heat, or whiteness, or any other manifestation, in this way: each of these is produced from motion simultaneously with the sensation of it, and intermediately between[1] the agent and the patient. The patient thus becomes sensitive,[2] but not sensation, and the agent becomes of a certain quality, but not the quality itself.[3]

---

[1] Or, ‘by the mutual relations of.’

[2] Reading αἰσθητὴν or αἰσθητικὸν for αἰσθητόν.

[3] *e. g.* the stone that strikes the sight becomes *white*, but is not *whiteness*, which *per se* does not exist. In what follows Plato derives the word ποιότης in

Perhaps then this word *quality* seems to you an outlandish term, and you do not understand it in its general sense. Well, then, hear about it in its several departments. The agent in such effect is not heat nor whiteness: it is only that a thing *becomes* hot, or white, and so on. For you remember, of course, that in our former discussion of this subject we stated the case thus :—that there is no self-existent *one*, nor any agent or patient taken alone, but that from both, united by a mutual relation, and so producing[1] the perceptions and the perceptible effects, the one kind of things become of a certain quality, and the other become sentient of it.

Theod. I remember that, of course.

Soc. Then let us dismiss all other considerations, and the inquiries whether things are so or not so, and keep strictly to the point which is the subject of our conversation, and put to them this question : You say, do you not, that all things have motion and flux ?

Theod. Just so.

Soc. And with both kinds of motion that we have distinguished, viz. motion in space, and alteration ?

Theod. Of course,—if they are to have a complete or perfect motion.

Soc. Well, now, if some things had only the former kind of motion, but not that of alteration, we should be able to say, I presume, what those things are that have the motion of flux.[2]

Theod. That is so.

Soc. But as not even this is permanent,[3] that what has flux should flow white, but it is ever changing, so that there

his playful way from ποιεῖν. Stallbaum remarks that this is the only Platonic passage in which the word is used, though it became so essential a term in later and in modern philosophy and science.

[1] We should read, I think, ἀποτικτόντων for ἀποτίκτοντα.

[2] Since the motion of ἀλλοίωσις would then be distinct.

[3] Since there is ἀλλοίωσις even in flux, as when we say a stream 'flows muddy,' though the state of muddiness must be undergoing change even while we pronounce the word. When we say 'milk flows white', or, 'white paint is getting brown,' etc., we predicate the *existence* of whiteness.

is also a flux of this very quality, the whiteness, and a change
to some other colour (that it may not be found stationary in
this respect[1]), is it possible at any given time to describe anything as of a particular colour, so as to give it a right name?

Theod. How can that be, Socrates, or anything else of the
like kind, if it is always passing away while one names it,[2] as
being in a state of flux?

Soc. What then are we to say about perception of any
kind, as that of seeing or hearing? Does it ever remain in
the precise act of seeing or hearing?   E

Theod I suppose it ought not, as *every* thing is in a state
of motion.[3]

Soc. Then we must not say that we see a thing any more
than that we don't see it; nor that we have any other perception rather than not, if, as we affirm, all things move in all
ways.

Theod. No, indeed.

Soc. But perception is knowledge, as both I and Theætetus
contended.

Theod. It was so.

Soc. Then our answer to the question, What is knowledge?
amounted to this; that it is non-knowledge just as much as it
is knowledge.

Theod. That seems to be the answer you gave.   183

Soc. Then our attempt to improve on the answer will
prove not very successful, when we try to demonstrate that all
things are in motion, in order that that reply[4] may seem a
correct one. For on the contrary it has been shown that, on
the theory of all things in motion, every answer, on whatever
subject one may give it, is equally right whether it says it is so

---

[1] This is playfully said, as if the doctrine of the στασιῶται were rejected and
refuted even by inanimate nature.

[2] For a current, to be a current at all, cannot have even a momentary check.

[3] Including therefore even the sense of seeing, etc.

[4] That αἴσθησις is ἐπιστήμη. If there is nothing stable to perceive, there is
no perception, and if there is no perception there is no knowledge.

or it is not so,—or, if you please, *becomes* so, that we may not
make them[1] the advocates of 'fixedness' by using the term 'is.'

Theod. You say rightly.

Soc. Except indeed, Theodore, that I said 'so' and 'not
so'; for when we apply either term to anything, it ceases to be
in motion, since not even 'it is not so' allows of motion. No !   B
we must establish some other kind of language for those who
assert this doctrine, since at present they have no phrases in
accordance with their own hypothesis, unless indeed 'not at
all';[2] such a phrase might suit them best, being quite indefinite
in its meaning.

Theod. Certainly this sort of talk is most suited to them.

Soc. Then now, Theodore, we have got rid of your friend
Protagoras, and at present we refuse to concede to him that
every man is the measure of every thing, unless he be in-   C
telligent. We shall not allow that knowledge is perception,
at least on the theory of universal motion; unless Theætetus
here has anything to say on the other side.[3]

Theod. You have spoken very well, Socrates; for now that
we have come to these conclusions, I also[4] ought to be let off
from replying to you, according to the agreements we made
when the argument about Protagoras' doctrine should have
come to an end.

XXIX. *Theæt.* No, Theodore, no ! not till you and   D
Socrates have fully discussed the views of those who maintain
on the other hand that the universe stands still. For this, you
know, you lately agreed to do.

Theod. What, Theætetus ! You, a young man, teach your

---

[1] αὐτοὺς refers to τοὺς ἀποκρινομένους implied in περὶ ὅτου ἄν τις ἀποκρί-
νηται.

[2] He ironically suggests an indefinite formula in place of the definite οὕτως.

[3] Of course, if all things are in perpetual flux, it is a fallacy to say we
perceive an object to be white, since at the very moment of the fancied perception, it is changing. Yet this very fact, τὸ πάντα κινεῖσθαι, was taken as
a proof that each man's perception at any moment *is* his knowledge.

[4] In allusion to τοῦ σοῦ ἑταίρου ἀπηλλάγμεθα.

G

seniors to be dishonest by breaking their promises![1] No; make up your mind to give Socrates your views on the subject that still remains.[2]

Theæt. I will, if he wishes it: but I should have liked best to hear rather than to reply about the subject I speak of.

Theod. You challenge cavalry into the open field,[3] Theætetus, in challenging Socrates to a conversation. Do you therefore put your questions to him and you shall hear him.

Soc. But I don't think, Theodore, that I shall do as Theætetus bids me in the matter he proposes to question me about.　　E

Theod. Why shall you not do so?

Soc. Because I feel a sort of awe of Melissus and those others who assert that the universe stands still, and a fear lest we should consider their doctrine in an undignified way.[4] And yet I fear them less than I do Parmenides, though they are many and he is one. But to me Parmenides appears (to quote the words of Homer) at once to be respected and feared as an adversary. For I had an interview with that man, you must know, when I was very young and he was far advanced in life; and he appeared to me to display a depth that showed true 184 genius. I am afraid therefore that we may fail to understand his statements, and even yet more fail to perceive his real meaning in making them. Nay more, and what is most important, I fear that the subject which the argument has undertaken to discuss,—the question, what is knowledge,—will never be fully examined if so many topics keep pouring in upon us, and we comply with their demands upon our time. Besides, in addition to other considerations, the subject we are now mooting is endless in its bearings and aspects; and if one is to treat

---

[1] Theodore was to be let off when he had discussed the question, if every man can be as wise as every other, p. 169. A, C.

[2] That of στάσις opposed to κίνησις.

[3] A proverb applied to the requesting others to do just what they most like, or what suits them best.

[4] By making sport of it. He means, that Parmenides is a formidable adversary, and one not easily refuted Compare *Sophist.* p. 237. A, Παρμενίδης ὁ μέγας παισὶν μὲν οὖσιν—τοῦτο ἀπεμαρτύρατο.

it as of secondary importance, it would hardly meet with its deserts, while, if pursued fully, it must be protracted so as to put the primary question about knowledge quite out of sight. Now neither of these alternatives is right; we must rather try if we can deliver Theætetus, by our obstetric art, of the   B sentiments he entertains respecting knowledge.

Theod. Well, if such is your pleasure, we will take that course.

Soc. Then give your attention once more, Theætetus, to this point, in the subject we have discussed. You said in your answer that Perception was Knowledge. Was it not so?

Theat. Yes.

Soc. If then any one should put this question to you: By what does a person see black and white, and by what does he hear sounds of high or low pitch? you would reply, I suppose, By his eyes and his ears.

Theat. I should.

Soc. Well, this off-hand use of words and phrases, when   C not put to the test of accuracy, is, in general, rather a mark of good breeding, as the contrary is pedantic. Nevertheless, it is sometimes necessary, just as now we are compelled to take hold of the answer you give, in so far as it is not correct. For consider: which is the more correct answer, that the organ *by* which we see is the eye, or *through* which we see? And similarly with the ear,—do we hear by or through it?

Theæt. It seems to me, Socrates, that our senses are rather the means than the instruments of perception.

Soc. Why, I should say it would be rather strange, my   D dear boy, if many distinct senses reside in us,[1] as if we were so many wooden horses, instead of all these sensations centering in some one faculty, whether it be soul or whatever we are to call it, *by* which we perceive whatever is perceptible, *through* these senses as through instruments.

----

[1] It would be strange if one has half-a-dozen or more distinct, isolated, and independent faculties, called senses, resident in us, rather than some one intellectual mode of apprehension.

Theæt. Well, I think it is in this way rather than in that other.

Soc. Now why do I give you this accurate distinction? It is to inquire whether there be not some one and the same principle in us all by which we realize black or white through the medium of the eyes, and other sensations through other organs; and whether, if asked, you will be able to refer *all*   E such impressions to the body alone? And perhaps it is better for *you* to give your views about them by way of answer, than that I should be so very particular in your behoof. And now tell me: Do you not assign to the body all the several faculties by which you perceive hot, or hard, or light, or sweet things; or do you think they belong to something else?[1]

Theæt. To nothing else.

Soc. Will you also be willing to admit, that what you ˙ perceive through one faculty it is impossible to perceive through another,—for instance, through seeing you cannot get the 185 impressions you do from hearing, or through hearing, those of seeing?

Theæt. Of course I shall allow that.

Soc. Then, if you have any mental conception about both, you would not be said to have a sensible perception of that through either organ, any more than you would have of both through only one.[2]

Theæt. Certainly not.

Soc. Well, now, on the subject of voice and colour, in the first place you have this idea about both, that they have being.

Theæt. I do.

---

[1] The argument is, that as there must be a mental faculty, beyond and beside the mere organ of sense, which takes cognisance of and reasons on effects; therefore mere αἴσθησις is not enough to account for knowledge, *i. e* without the reasoning power that in man seems inseparable from sense. Compare *Sophist.* p. 248. A, σώματι μὲν ἡμᾶς γενέσει δι' αἰσθήσεως κοινωνεῖν, διὰ λογισμοῦ δὲ ψυχῇ πρὸς τὴν ὄντως οὐσίαν. Where γένεσιν means passing or transient impressions as opposed to τὰ ὄντως ὄντα, abstract and eternal existences. See also *Phaedo*, p. 73—74, where the first germ of this doctrine appears.

[2] There must be some mental impression different from the merely physical.

Soc. Also that each is different from each, but the same as itself?[1]

Theæt. Of course.

B

Soc. And that both make two, and each is one?

Theæt. That also is true.

Soc. Well, are you not also able to make up your mind whether they are alike or unlike to each other?

Theæt. Perhaps.

Soc. Then through what faculty do you entertain all these notions about them? For it is not possible to realize any common property respecting them either by hearing or by sight. And there is this further proof of what we assert: if the question could reasonably be asked about both, Have they any salt in them or not? you are aware that you would be able to state with what faculty you would put this to the test;   C
and that proves to be neither sight nor hearing, but something different.

Theæt. Why, of course it is, being the faculty we have through the tongue.

Soc. Well said. But through what comes the faculty that makes known to you the common property of all[2] and the special property of each,—what you call the Being or the non-Being, and the other properties[3] of them that we just now inquired about? What organs or intruments will you assign to all these, as the means by which our sentient faculty has perception of them severally?

Theæt. You mean their Being or non-Being, likeness and unlikeness, their identity or difference, their oneness or any other number they may possess. It is plain, too, that your   D
question refers to oddness or evenness, and other conditions of that kind;—you want to know through which of the bodily faculties we obtain a mental conception of these things.

[1] Sound is sound, and colour is colour, in spite of the difference in kind of each. This is the doctrine of 'otherness' discussed in the *Sophistes*. We are intellectually conscious that stone is not bread, that earth is not water, etc.

[2] Viz. the οὐσία, or Being.

[3] The otherness or the identity of them.

Soc. You follow my meaning admirably, Theætetus; what I ask is precisely this.

Theæt. Upon my word, then, Socrates, I couldn't tell you; but this I can say, that there does not seem to me to be any special organ at all of this nature, as there is to those other sensible impressions. It appears to me that the soul by its own efforts takes into consideration the *common* properties in all   E these cases.

Soc. Indeed, Theætetus, you are a good looking fellow, and not, as Theodore said of you, plain-featured. For one who says well is well-mannered and well born and bred. And besides your good replies you have done me good by ridding me of a great deal of talk, if you say that the soul examines some points by itself, and others through means of the bodily faculties. That was the very opinion I held myself; but I wanted you to hold it too.

Theæt. Well, that certainly is my idea of the matter.   186

XXX. *Soc.* To which of these faculties then[1] do you refer the Being of the objects of our impressions? For this is the first and chief consideration in them all.

Theæt. For my part, I refer it to those conceptions which the soul by itself tries to attain to.

Soc. Do you refer to the same, the likeness or unlikeness, the identity or difference of them?

Theæt. Yes.

Soc. What are we say of their fairness or foulness, their goodness or badness?

Theæt. It appears to me that these are matters of which the soul in an especial manner considers the Being in their mutual relations, by drawing analogies in itself between the   B past, the present, and the future.[2]

---

[1] To the bodily perception, or the mental conception?

[2] The soul considers *will* this be right, comparing it with what *is* or *was* right, *i e.* was proved by the result to be right, on some former occasion. Many questions of casuistry, the οὐσία of καλὸν or αἰσχρὸν, depend on this for their solution.

Soc. Stay, now. Is it not through the touch that the soul must get a perception of the hardness of what is hard, and likewise of the softness of what is soft?

Theæt It is.

Soc. But the *existence* of such qualities as hardness or softness, their nature, and their antagonism to each other, and again, the existence of such antagonism, the soul endeavours to determine for us without any external aid, by gradually attaining these notions and by comparing the one with the other.[1]

Theæt. Certainly it does

Soc. Some of these effects then, I mean those which reach the soul through the medium of the body, are felt at their very birth, by the instinct of nature, by both man and animals; but   C the reasonings about them, in respect of their existence and their use, come only by time and through much trouble and instruction, to such as do attain to them at all.

Theæt. That is undoubtedly the case.

Soc. Is it possible then for anyone to get to the truth, if he has not realised the fact of existence?

Theæt. It is not.

Soc. And if one misses the true view of anything, will he ever have a correct knowledge of it?

Theæt. Of course not, Socrates   D

Soc Then it is not in the feelings produced that real knowledge consists, but in the reasoning about them. For in this, as it appears, it *is* possible to realize Being and Truth, whereas in mere perception it is impossible.

Theæt. It seems so.

Soc. Do you then call conception the same as perception, when there are such differences between the two?

Theæt. Not in fairness, at least.

Soc What name then do you assign to the latter,—I mean the seeing, hearing, smelling, or the feeling of getting warm or cold?

[1] Questions of fact are generally determined by sense, but moral and metaphysical questions by analogy or induction

Theæt. I call it tho having a sense of such effects : what E
other name can I give it?

Soc. Then you call it by the general term *sensation*?

Theat. I have no better term for it.

Soc. But that, we say, is unable to get at truth, since it
cannot realize Being?

Theæt. It cannot.

Soc. And therefore not knowledge either?

Theæt. No.

Soc. Then, Theætetus, perception and exact knowledge
never can be the same.

Theæt. It appears not, Socrates; and by this argument
more plainly than by any other it has become manifest that
knowledge is something different from sensation.

Soc. Yes; but surely it was not for this that wo began our
conversation, that we might discover what knowledge is not, 187
but that we might know what it is. However, wo have made
so much progress, as no longer to look for it in sensation at all,
but in that property of the soul, whatever name it may have,
when by its own reasonings it concerns itself with the nature
of things that exist.

Theæt. But surely, Socrates, that is called, if I mistake
not, 'forming an opinion.'

Soc. You think rightly, my friend; and now consider
again from the beginning, after wiping clean from your mind
all previous impressions, whether you get any clearer view B
now that you have advanced to this point. And first tell me
again, what knowledge is.

XXXI. *Theæt.* To call it opinion generally, Socrates, is
impossible, since there is such a thing as false opinion But it
seems likely that true opinion is knowledge; and let that be
my answer for the present. For if it should appear not to be
so, as we go on, as it now does appear, we will then try to give
some other definition.

Soc. That is the right way to speak, Theætetus, with a
hearty earnestness, rather than with the timidity you showed

at first in replying. For if we do this, we shall gain one of two things,—either we shall get hold of what we are going after, or we shall be less disposed to think that we know what C we don't know: and such a return as that for our trouble is not to be thought lightly of. And so now what say you? There being two kinds of opinion, one that is true[1] and the other that is false, do you define knowledge to be true opinion?[2]

Theæt. I do; that is the view I now incline to.

Soc. Is it not then worth our while to take up again and discuss the question of opinion?

Theæt. What particular question do you allude to?

Soc. One which[3] some how or other gives me anxiety now, as it has done often before; so that I have been in great perplexity in considering it not only with myself, but with others, D from not being able to define what this feeling is, and how it is produced in us.

Theæt. What feeling?

Soc. One's having a *false* opinion. Hence I am even now in doubt whether we should let it pass, or consider it in some other way than we did shortly before.

Theæt. Of course we should, Socrates, if there seems even the smallest need for doing so. Only just now you and Theodore said well about leisure, that in matters of this kind[4] there is nothing to hurry us.

Soc. You are right in reminding me. Perhaps it will not E be out of place to pursue the question as one would hunt on a track. For, of course, it is better to get through a small matter well than a great subject insufficiently.

Theæt. Certainly.

Soc. Well, then, what have we to say about it? Do we

---

[1] Lit. 'one that is the genuine kind, (the right sort,) the other the sham (or counterfeit) kind.'

[2] Lit. 'do you lay down as a definition that true opinion is knowledge?'

[3] I suggest ὃ θράττει μέ πως, etc , where the ὃ has dropped out of the MSS. from the similarity of the Θ following.

[4] Opposed to τοῖς δικανικοῖς, sup. p 172. C.

affirm that an opinion may sometimes be false, and that some
of us hold false, others true views, such being our natures
respectively ?

Theæt. We do maintain that.

Soc. Is there not then this alternative for us in all subjects 188
and severally in each, that we either know or do not know it ?
For of learning and forgetting, as intermediate between knowing and not knowing, I say nothing at present, since it has
nothing to do with the subject now.

Theæt. Well, then, Socrates, there is nothing left for it but
either to know or not to know on every subject.

Soc. It becomes necessary then that a man who forms an
opinion should form it on something which he either does or
does not know.

Theæt. It must be so.

Soc. But surely it is alike impossible for one who knows
something not to know it, and for one who does not know to   B
know it.

Theæt Of course.

Soc. Then, this being granted, does he who holds false
opinions think that what he knows is not this, but something
else of what he knows, and thus, while he knows both, is he
also in ignorance about both ?[1]

Theæt. Why, that would be impossible, Socrates.

Soc. Then does he imagine what he does *not* know to be
some other of the things he does not know ? That would be,
for one who does not know either Socrates or Theætetus by
sight, to take it into his head that either Socrates is Theætetus,
or Theætetus Socrates

Theæt. How can that possibly be ?   C

Soc. Well, surely, a man does not think that what he
knows is what he does not know,[2] nor, on the other hand, that
what he does not know is what he knows.

----

[1] *i e.* he knows them, but does not know the distinction between them, as
when he mistakes a sheep for a goat

[2] *e. g.* he cannot mistake a sheep for some creature he has never seen even in

Theæt. That would be marvellous, indeed.

Soc. Then what way remains in which one can have a false opinion? For beyond the limits I have mentioned it is impossible to have an opinion at all, since there can be nothing that we do not either know or not know; and it has been shown that in none of *these* is it possible to have false opinions.

Theæt. Very true.

Soc. Perhaps then, in considering the question before us, we must not pursue the track of knowledge and non-knowledge, D but that of Being and non-Being.[1]

Theæt. How is that?

Soc. We must consider whether it be not simply true, that one who thinks that something possesses qualities that it has not,[2] must of necessity have a *false* opinion, however correct his general views may be.

Theæt. Why, that again appears likely, Socrates.

Soc. What then? What are we to say, Theætetus, if some one should put this question: Is what we are speaking of possible to any one,—that is, can any human being ever conceive *what is not*, either abstractedly or about any existing thing? Well, we, I suppose, shall reply to this, ' Yes, when, in holding an opinion he holds what is not true.' Or how must we state the case? E

Theæt. As you have.

Soc. Is then such a thing as this possible in other faculties beside thought?

Theæt. As what?

---

a picture. But the next alternative does not seem impossible: a man may mistake A, whom he has never seen, for B, whom he knows intimately. See below, p. 191. B.

[1] As in the *Sophistes*, p. 127, seqq For the form of expression compare Eur. *Ion* 1090, κατὰ μοῦσαν ἰόντας.

[2] *e.g.* that a ball or an apple has hardness or softness, which may be deceptive to the touch. The argument is, that a man must think something, if he thinks at all; but *something* has existence, and therefore δοξάζειν μὴ ὄντα is impossible.

Soc. As this, I mean, if a man sees something and yet sees nothing.

Theæt. Of course it is not.

Soc. Yet, surely, if he sees some *one* object, he sees something of things that exist. Or do *you* think that this ' one' is sometimes among things non-existent?

Theæt. No, *I* do not.

Soc. Then he who sees one object sees a thing that does exist.

Theæt. It appears so.

Soc. And so a person who hears must hear some one sound, and therefore an effect that is real.

Theæt. Yes.

Soc. And he who touches something touches some one object, 189 and by consequence some object that actually exists.

Theæt. That too may be granted.

Soc. But does not he who forms an opinion form it about something?

Theæt. He must do so.

Soc. And if about *one* thing, then about an *existing* thing?

Theæt. I grant that.

Soc. Then a man who thinks that which is not, thinks nothing.[1]

Theæt. It seems so.

Soc. But surely one who ' thinks nothing' does not think at all !

Theæt. That must be so, as it seems.

Soc. It is not possible, then to think what is not, either about existing things, or in the abstract.

Theæt. It appears not.

Soc. Then holding false opinions is something different from believing what is not.

Theæt. It does seem different.

---

[1] *i. e.* not ψευδῆ δοξάζει, but οὐδ' ἓν (οὐδὲν) δοξάζει. For ὁ ὅν τι δοξάζων ἕν τι δοξάζει.

Soc. Then neither according to this view nor according to the line of argument[1] we just before pursued, is there any such thing as false opinion in us.

Theæt. I quite see that there is not.

XXXII. *Soc.* Then must we call it 'false opinion' as taking place in some such way as this?

Theæt. How?

Soc. Must we say that false opinion is an 'allodoxy'; by which I mean, when a man affirms that something of what really exists is something else of what really exists, mistaking C in his mind the one for the other? For, according to this view, he does always think what is, only one thing in place of another; and thus, being wrong in the subject of his inquiry, he might properly be said to hold a false opinion.

Theæt. Now you seem to me to have spoken most correctly. For when, for instance, a man thinks something is bad instead of good, or good instead of bad, then he truly thinks what is false.

Soc. It is evident, Theætetus, that you have a contempt for me, and hold me in no fear.

Theæt. Why in the world do you say that?

Soc. I suppose you think I shall not object to that expression 'truly false', by asking you if it is possible for quick to D take place slowly, or light heavily, or any other contrary not according to its own nature, but according to that of its opposite, and so in a way contrary to itself. This little matter, however, I will not dwell upon, that you may have some real ground for encouragement. But you accept, as you say, the view, that to have a false opinion is to think one thing instead of another?

Theæt. Yes, I do.

Soc. In your opinion then it is possible 'to take in one's apprehension one thing for another thing, and not for what the former thing really is.'

Theæt. That is just it.

---

[1] Viz εἰδέναι καὶ μή.

Soc. Then whenever one's mind performs this act, must it   E
not also think about both, or at all events about one?

Theæt. That is necessary.

Soc. Either at once, or in turn?

Theæt. Precisely.

Soc. Now do you mean what I do by this work *thinking*?

Theæt. What do you call it?

Soc. I call it 'a reasoning-process, which the soul goes
through with itself about the subject it may be considering',—
to deliver an opinion to you without full knowledge.[1] That
is what it seems to me to do in thinking,—nothing else than to
converse, questioning and answering itself, affirming this or 190
denying that, and when at length, after determining it more
or less quickly, by taking a survey and applying itself to the
task,[2] it says the same about it and no longer doubts, we take
this as its *opinion*. So that I call the forming an opinion
a kind of affirming, and an opinion, a discourse spoken, not
indeed to another, nor in audible words, but silently to oneself. What say *you*?

Theæt. I agree.

Soc. Whenever then a person thinks one thing is another
thing, then he also asserts to himself that this is that.

Theæt. Of course.   B

Soc. Recal to mind now whether you ever said to yourself,
as in the form of a maxim, that, beyond a doubt, 'Fair is foul',
or, 'Wrong is right'; or, (to sum up every such case under
one general head,) consider whether you ever tried to persuade
yourself that beyond a doubt one thing is some other thing; or,
on the contrary, never even in a dream went so far as to say to
yourself that assuredly[3] these odd numbers are even, or anything
of that kind.

---

[1] We should read ἀποφαίνωμαι, not ἀποφαίνομαι.

[2] 'Going *at* it,' in familiar phrase. So Hom. *Il.* xv 80, ὡς δ' ὅταν ἀΐξῃ
νόος ἀνέρος. The meaning is, that δόξα is an act of deliberation, and does not
admit of the casual mistaking one thing for another.

[3] The emphasis on παντὸς μᾶλλον, παντάπασιν, and (inf.) ἀνάγκη, must be

Theæt. The truth is as you have last put it.

Soc. And do you suppose that anyone beside yourself,   C
either in sound health or out of his mind, seriously said to
himself, and with the intention of persuading himself, that that
ox *must* be a horse, or these two *must* be one?

Theæt. I don't think so, upon my word.

Soc. Then, if saying to oneself means forming an opinion,
no one, in speaking of or thinking of both of two things, and
realizing both in his mind, would be likely to say or think
that one was the other; indeed, you will have to give up the
very phrase 'other',[1] for I put the proposition thus: 'No man
thinks that foul is fair', or anything of the like contrary nature.   D

Theæt. Yes, Socrates, I resign 'other', as you say, and
I agree with you.

Soc. Then, in having an opinion about both, he cannot
think that one is the other.

Theæt. So it seems.

Soc. But surely if he thinks only about one, and not at all
about the other, he will never think that the one is the other.

Theæt. That is true; he would then be obliged to realize
that which he has no opinion about.

Soc. Then one cannot have "allodoxy' in thinking of *both*
any more than in thinking of *one* of two things. So that,   E
if one shall define false opinion to mean 'thinking this is
that', he will hardly say what is much to the purpose, since it
has been shown there cannot be such a thing as 'false opinion'
according to this, any more than according to the former
views [2]

Theæt. It seems not.

XXXIII. *Soc.* But surely, Theætetus, if it shall appear

---

noticed. The argument requires, not a doubt whether black may be white, but
a positive assertion that black *is* white. For a δόξα is formed only on the
cessation of doubt; it is the conclusion you have arrived at.

[1] Mr. Jowett refers to *Parmen.* p. 147. C. The simple sense may be, "No
one would think A was B,—I need not say, that B was A."

[2] Viz. of the non-knowledge and the non-being.

that there really is no such thing, we shall be compelled to make many strange admissions.

Theæt. Of what kind?

Soc. I won't tell you, till I have considered and tried the question in all its bearings. For I should feel ashamed for us if, while our doubts are yet upon us,[1] we should feel ourselves forced to make such concessions as I speak of. No! when we have found the truth and have become free, we shall then be 191 able to speak of those others as having to bear it,[2] while we ourselves stand clear of ridicule. If, however, we find ourselves perplexed after all our efforts, then, I suppose, we must submit to be humbled, and give ourselves up to the argument, like sea-sick voyagers, to trample on us and treat us as it pleases. Hear therefore the one way that I can find for bringing this inquiry to an end.[3]

Theæt. You have only to say it.

Soc. I shall say that we were wrong in allowing some time ago that it is impossible for a man to think, that what he knows is something that he does not know, and so to be mis-   B taken about it: on the contrary, I shall contend that in a certain sense it is possible.

Theæt. Do you mean (what I surmised at the time when you said it) that there may be a mistake of this kind: I, on some occasion, knowing Socrates, and seeing at a distance some one else, whom I do not, fancied that 'this is the Socrates whom I know'? For certainly in such a case what you speak of does occur.

Soc. We gave up the question then because it seemed to make us at once to know what we know and not to know it.[4]

Theæt. Certainly.

---

[1] *i. e.* before every method has been tried for removing them.

[2] πασχόντων, viz. γελοίων ὄντων. Those who deny there is such a thing as false opinion will be driven into difficulties which *we* hope to avoid. The simplest and best reading seems to be αὐτοὶ ἐκτὸς τοῦ γελοίου ἑστῶτες.

[3] *i. e.* for showing that ψευδὴς δόξα is possible.

[4] Whereas εἰδότα μὴ εἰδέναι ἀδύνατον, sup. p. 188. B.

Soc. Then don't let us put it so, but in the following way: and perhaps it will fall in with our present view, or perhaps it will still hold out in opposition. But the fact is, we are caught C in such a strait that it has become necessary to turn every argument[1] and put it to the test. Consider, therefore, whether there is anything in what I say. Is it possible for one who did not know something before, to learn it afterwards?

Theæt. It is, of course.

Soc. And also another thing afterwards, and again another? *Theæt.* Certainly.

Soc. Assume then, for the sake of argument, that there is in our souls a waxen tablet for receiving impressions,—in one of us a greater, in another a less; in one, of purer, in another, of unclarified wax; in some harder, in some softer, in others, D of medium quality.

Theæt. I assume that.

Soc. Let us further say that it was the gift of the mother of the Muses, Memory[2]; and that upon this tablet, whenever we desire to remember something that we have seen or heard or conceived the idea of in our own thoughts, we take off an impression, by holding it under our sensations or thoughts, just as when we take the impression of gems in our rings.[3] Thus, whatever is taken off on the tablet, that we remember and know, so long as the form remains in our minds; but when it has been effaced, or cannot be taken off at all, then we forget and do not know it. E

Theæt. That is so.

Soc. Observe now whether a person who is considering

---

[1] Probably a metaphor from wall-building. By λόγον μεταστρέφειν he may mean the putting of an old argument in a new or altered form.

[2] Μνήμης ἁπάντων μουσομήτορ' ἐργάνην, Æsch. *Prom.* 469,—a verse which shows how little the idea of a *written* literature (if it existed at all) prevailed at that time.

[3] These gems, from their minute cutting, are called θριπήδεστα σφραγίδια, 'worm-eaten seals,' in Ar. *Thesm.* 427. In the same play, 514, we have αὐτέκμαγμα, 'an exact impression.'

something of what he sees or hears, and therefore with a knowledge of it, can be said to have a false opinion about it in some such way as this.

Theæt. In what way?

Soc. By thinking that what he knows is at one time what he knows, at another time what he does not. For we were wrong in our former argument[1] when we said this was impossible.

Theæt. Then how do you state the case now?

Soc. It should be stated[2] thus in the cases in question, and   192 a new distinction must be made between them. First, 'if a man knows something, and has the remembrance of it in his mind, but not a sensible perception; he cannot possibly think it to be something else of what he knows, while he retains the impression of this latter, but has not at the time a perception of it '[3]   Secondly, it is equally impossible for a man to think that what he knows is something that he does not know and has no impression of at all.[4]   Or, that what he does not know is some other thing that he does not know,[5] or, what he does not know is something that he does know[6]; or, to think that what he has a sensible perception of, is some other thing which he also knows by his senses; or, that what he *has* a sense of is something that he has *not* a sense of[7]; or, what he has not a sense of is something else that he has not a sense of; or,   B what he has not a sense of, is something he *has* a sense of. We may go yet further, and say it is yet more impossible (if that can be) to think that what one *both* knows and feels,

<hr />

[1] Sup. p. 188. C, ἀλλ' οὐ μὴν, ἅ γε τις οἶδεν, οἴεταί που ἃ μὴ οἶδεν αὐτὰ εἶναι.

[2] Probably we should read διαλέγεσθαι, or at least, διοριζομένοις.

[3] *e. g.* if he knows from observation, that acorns grow on oaks and crabs on crab-trees, he cannot think that acorns grow on crab-trees   But inf p 196, a case of this kind is shown to be possible, *i. e.* when abstract ideas are concerned

[4] As that an acorn is a crab, which he has never seen or tasted.

[5] *e. g.* that an oyster is a whelk, when he has seen neither. This is the *third* case, p. 193 A.

[6] As that a crab-apple is an acorn.

[7] That a stick which he sees is a stone which he does not see. (The cases now given merely *substitute* 'sense', *i. e.* perception, for 'knowledge.')

and also has an impression of in accordance with the feeling,[1]
is something else that one knows and feels and has an impies-
sion of as well as of the other, and according also to one's
feeling.[2] It is also impossible, when one knows something
and perceives it, and retains a right impression of it, to think
it something else that one knows[3]; or, that what one knows
and feels also with right impression, is something else that one
feels; or, what one neither knows nor feels, is something else
of what one neither knows nor feels: or, what one neither
knows nor feels, is what one does not know; or, what one   C
neither knows nor feels, is what one does not feel.[4]   All these
are cases where it is in the highest degree impossible to have a
false opinion in any of them. It remains, therefore, that in such
cases as the following, if anywhere, false opinion may occur.

Theæt. And what cases are these? Tell me, if perchance
I derive some further knowledge from them[5]; for at present
I don't follow you.

Soc. In the cases where a man knows certain things or
objects, he may think them some other of what he knows and
has a present perception of; or, secondly, of what he does *not*
know but yet has a perception of, or, lastly, where he thinks
that what he knows and feels is something else that he knows
and feels.

Theæt. Now I am left still further behind you than I was
before.   D

XXXIV. *Soc.* Then hear the case put in the reverse way.[6]

---

[1] Or, "by sensation"

[2] *e g.* that a lute is the same as a spade, both being present to you, and both
familiar objects as to their use and shape.

[3] This corresponds with the clause δ μέν τις οἶδεν, ἔχων αὐτοῦ μνημεῖον ἐν
τῇ ψυχῇ,—τοῦτο οἰηθῆναι ἕτερόν τι ὧν οἶδεν. (The cases now given *add* sense,
i. e. perception, to knowledge)

[4] If a man does not know nor feel either rheumatism or tooth-ache, he
cannot mistake one for the other.

[5] Or, 'out of the number of them '

[6] In *Phædr* p. 264, A, ἀνάπαλιν means 'backwards'. The sense here seems
to be that the illustration now comes before the general proposition.

I, knowing Theodore, and retaining in my mind the impression of what he is like, and Theætetus also in the same way, sometimes have the opportunity of seeing, touching, hearing, or by some other of my senses being aware of your presence, while sometimes I have not; and yet I remember you none the less, and so *know* you in my own consciousness.[1] Is it not so?

Theæt. Certainly.   E

Soc. Understand this then as the first point in what I wish to explain,—that it is possible either to have or not to have a perception through the senses of what one knows.

Theæt. True.

Soc. Is it not also possible that what one does *not* know one may, if so be, not perceive by sense at all, or one may *only* so perceive it?

Theæt. That also may happen.

Soc. See then if you follow me any better now.   Socrates knows at sight both Theodore and Theætetus, but actually sees 193 neither, and has no other perception of either. I say that he is not likely ever to form an opinion in his own thoughts that Theætetus is Theodore. Is there any truth in what I say?

Theæt. Yes, that is certainly true.   ·

Soc. This then is the first of the cases I put to you just now.[2]

Theæt. It is.

Soc. And the second is, that, knowing one of you and not the other, and having a present sense of neither,[3] again I should hardly think that the one whom I know is the other whom I do not.

Theæt. Rightly said.

----

[1] This is a case of ἐπιστήμη without αἴσθησις, whence the inference is, that ἐπιστήμη cannot be the same as αἴσθησις.

[2] P. 192. A, and (sup. D.) τοτὲ δ' αἴσθησιν μὲν οὐδεμίαν ἔχω περὶ ὑμῶν κ.τ.λ. As one may see or not see an object one knows, so one may see only (i. e. without knowledge) or not see what one does not know.

[3] Sup. E., ἃ μὴ οἶδε ἔστι μηδὲ αἰσθάνεσθαι. All that was here stated was the possibility of not perceiving by sense what one does not know. (If you don't know A, but *do* see him, you may mistake him for B, whom you know.)

Soc The third is, that if I neither know nor perceive either, I am not likely to think that one whom I don't know is another whom I don't know. I need not repeat to you all **B** the cases I mentioned before, in which I affirmed that I can never have a 'false opinion' about you and Theodore; whether I know or do not know you both, or know one and not the other. You must suppose you have heard them all stated again in the same order. And what I say about the senses generally you must understand in the same way, if you follow my meaning

Theæt. I do.

Soc. There remains then only this case in which we can have a false opinion. ' I know you and Theodore; I retain in the waxen tablet I spoke of the impressions of you both, as if they **C** had been stamped on it by seals. Well, at some distance, and so not with sufficient clearness, I see you both together; and I make an effort, in assigning the proper mark of each to the particular sight[1] of him, to put the sense of sight exactly upon its seal-mark, that I may thence obtain a mental recognition. But I fail in my efforts,[2] and, like persons who put a right shoe on the left foot, I take one for the other, and apply my sight of one to my mental impression of the other; or, as happens to objects seen in a mirror, which causes the right sides to pass into the left,[3] I have a change taking place in me, **D** and so get wrong as to the identity.' In this case then occurs the 'allodoxy' that we spoke of, and so the having a false opinion.

Theæt. Why, Socrates, what happens to one's opinion is marvellously like what you describe.

Soc. Further than this, there may be mistaken opinion when I know both of two persons, and of one, besides the knowledge, I have also the perception,[4] but not the perception

---

[1] Or, 'to the sight belonging to that mark.'

[2] Lit. 'missing these impressions.'

[3] It seems that μεταρρεῖν is here active

[4] The οἶδα καὶ αἰσθάνομαι of p 192 B. A man knows A and B, and sees only A. Then he may mistake him for B.

of the other, and so have knowledge of *him* not in the way of actual perception. This is a case which I put before, and you did not then seem to understand me.

Theæt. I did not.

Soc. Well, I meant this: Knowing the one, and also perceiving him,—that is, having a knowledge of him by perception,[1]   E —one can never think that he is another of those whom he knows and perceives, *i. e.* if he has a knowledge of *him* too by perception. Was it not so?

Theæt. It was.

Soc. But we then omitted the particular case we now describe,—that false opinion may occur when a man knows and sees both persons, or has any other kind of perception of them both, but has the mental impression of each not agreeing with the actual perception.[2] For then he is like a bad archer 194 who hits a wrong mark in shooting and so misses; which is what we call deception.

Theæt. That is a likely view of the case.

Soc. And further, when there is present perception to one of the impressions, but not to the other, and when a person applies the mental impression of the object of which he has not a present sense to that of which he has,[3] in this way the mind is also quite deceived. To put the matter quite briefly: where a man has no knowledge and never had any perception of an object, he cannot, as it seems, be deceived, and there can be no   B false opinion,[4]—that is, if there is any truth in the views we

---

[1] By κατὰ αἴσθησιν he means that the knowledge coincides with the impression on the memory, sup. p. 192. B., ὧν ἔχει τὸ σημεῖον κατὰ τὴν αἴσθησιν.

[2] *e. g.* he had forgotten that it was A who had white hair, and not B.   Lit. ' when he has the two impressions, not of A according with the sight of A, nor of B according with the sight of B.'   But the true reading is probably τὸ σημεῖον μὴ κατὰ τὴν αὐτοῦ αἴσθησιν ἑκατέρου, 'according to his perception of each.'

[3] When his recollections of A, whom he does not see, are wrongly applied to those of B, whom he does see.   This frequently happens: we mistake A for B, because we thought it was A who wore that particular dress, etc.

[4] For there is no mental σημεῖον about such persons at all, and therefore no ground or scope for mistake about them.

are now putting forward. It is on objects that we both know and have perception of that opinion turns, and on these alone that it is engaged. And it becomes either false or true opinion accordingly as it is applied. If it brings the seal-mark and the impressions that belong to it right down upon and exactly opposite to the object seen,[1] then it is a true opinion; if aslant and sideways, then it is a false one.

Theæt. And is not this, Socrates, a very fair account of the matter?

Soc. You will say so still more when you hear the following C considerations; for the holding of truth *is* a fair, just as being in error is a foul thing.

Theæt. Of course.

Soc. Well, now, they tell us that truth and error result from these causes: when the wax in the mind's tablet is deep, and smooth, and there is plenty of it, and it is sufficiently softened, then the ideas that came upon us through the senses, leaving their marks on this heart's core, (as Homer called it, hinting at the resemblance of κέαρ to κηρὸς,)—then these impressions, being made clear and distinct, and deep enough, are D lasting, and persons who are so favoured by nature are in the first place apt at learning, secondly, they have good memories, and thirdly, they do not misapply the marks left by the sensations, but form true opinions. For as the marks are clear, and are not crowded, they at once assign each object to its proper place in their memory[2]; and then it is that we say impressions are really true, and men so constituted are wise men. Don't you think so?

Theæt. I do, decidedly.

Soc. And when one's heart has hairs in it,[3] (which, you E

---

[1] When your recollections of A as to face, dress, etc., are rightly applied to A when you see him, and not confounded with your recollections of B. The metaphor is derived from replacing a gem exactly upon the impression that has been taken of it.

[2] Construe διανέμουσιν ἕκαστα ἐπὶ τὰ αὐτῶν ἐκμαγεῖα.

[3] A hair in wax would interfere with the impression from a seal. Plato again plays on the Homeric phrase λάσιον κῆρ.

know, that all-wise poet referred to,) or when it is dirty and
not of pure wax, or very moist or very hard, then those who
have soft tablets learn easily indeed, but are apt to forget,
those who have hard, are slow to learn but retentive. Those
whose hearts[1] have hairs in, or are rough, or gritty, or full
of earth or dirt mixed up with them, have the impressions
made on their tablets indistinct, as those also have whose
tablets are hard,—for the impressions have no depth—or too
soft, for then they become obscure through so soon running
one into the other. And if, beside all these faults, the impres- 195
sions fall upon and interfere with each other through want of
space, and a man happens to be small-minded, in this case they
are still more indistinct than in the other. All these persons
then are likely to have false opinions; for whenever they hear
or see or conceive any idea, they are unable at the instant
to assign each to each,[2] but being slow and prone to put things
in their wrong places, they see wrongly, hear wrongly, think
wrongly about almost everything; and such persons we don't
call 'wise', but, on the contrary, mistaken as to what really is,
and uninformed.

Theæt. No man could possibly give a truer account of the
matter, Socrates.   B

Soc. Must we then affirm that there are such things in us
as "false opinions?"

Theæt. O, certainly!

Soc. And true opinions too?

Theæt. And true.

Soc. Do you think then that by this time it has been determined with sufficient certainty that, as a matter of fact, these
two kinds of opinion do exist?

Theæt. Most decidedly so.

XXXV. *Soc.* I am afraid, Theætetus, that a man who

---

[1] Using κέαρ playfully in the sense of κηρός.

[2] The impression of it to the right object. Dickens' character of "Mrs.
Nickleby" is a very good illustration of this class of confused thinkers, or non-
thinkers.

is a twaddler runs a good chance of really being a formidable
as well as a disagreeable character!

Theæt. Why so? In respect of what do you say this?

Soc. From a feeling of vexation at my own dulness and   C
twaddling, in the true sense of the word. For what else can a
man call it, when one drags words to and fro, unable, from
sheer stupidity, to be convinced, and so finds it hard to get
clear away from each subject of discussion?

Theæt. And pray at what do *you* feel vexed?

Soc. I am not only vexed, but even alarmed, when I think
what reply I shall give if some·one asks me, O Socrates, have
you really then discovered that false opinion does not consist
in the mutual relations either of the senses or the ideas, but in
the right application of the sense to the idea?[1] And I suppose   D
I shall answer, 'Yes',—piquing myself on the conviction that
we have really made a clever discovery.

Theæt. I do think, Socrates, that what we have now proved
is very creditable to us.

Soc. 'You mean, then,' (he will say,) 'that a man, *as
man,*[2]—that is, whom we only conceive, but do not see,—can
never be mistaken by us for a horse, which likewise we neither
see nor touch, but have only an idea of without any sensible
perception of it whatever?'—That, I suppose, I shall say is
what I mean.

Theæt And you will rightly reply.

Soc. 'What then?' he will say. 'Is it not clear, according   E
to your statement, that a man can never imagine the number
eleven, which he only thinks of, to be twelve, which again he
only thinks of?'—Come, now, do *you* give an answer.

Theæt. Well, I shall answer, that if one actually *saw* or
touched them, he might possibly think eleven things were
twelve; but that, if he only has these figures in his mind,
he never can form such opinions about them.

[1] See p. 193 C.
[2] Heindorf's reading αὐτὸν for αὖ τὸν seems clearly right. Compare
Aristotle's use of αὐτοάνθρωπος and αὐτοέκαστος for an *abstract* individuality.

Soc. What then? Do you suppose there ever was a man who, after proposing to himself for consideration *five* and *seven*, —I do not mean either seven or five *men*, or any concrete objects 196 of that kind, but the abstract notions of five and seven, which we said were impressed on the waxen tablets of our memories, and that there was no scope for false opinion about them,— I say, was there ever a man who considered these abstract numbers, saying to himself and asking himself, What total do they make? and replied to himself, on conviction, 'They make eleven,' while another, perhaps, said, 'Twelve'? Or do all the world both say and think that $7 + 5 = 12$?

Theæt. No, indeed; many fancy they make eleven. And, if one considers the question by taking a larger number, he B makes a still greater mistake. For I assume that you are speaking about number generally.

Soc. You are right in your surmise. And now consider: does anything else then happen than that you suppose the abstract numbers in your memory, twelve, are eleven?[1]

Theæt. That seems to be so.

Soc. Then it comes back to our original statement. When anyone has this happen to him, he thinks that what he knows is something else of what he also knows, which we said was impossible[2]; and, in fact, by this very argument we tried to force the conviction that there could be no false opinion, that C the same man might not be compelled at once to know and not to know the very same things.

Theæt. Most true.

Soc. Then we are bound to show that the having a false opinion is something else than the wrong application of mental conception to the perception of sense. For, if this were so, we never could be mistaken in our *mere* conceptions. But as it is, either there is no false opinion, or it is possible not to know

---

[1] Here is a case in which false opinion is shown to be possible without αἴσθησις. "Plato in the *Theætetus* does not deny the possibility of error, but only seeks to give a psychological explanation of its origin and *modus operandi*." —(*Mr. Cope on Grote's Criticisms*, p. 29.)

[2] P. 192, init.

what one knows. And which of these paradoxes do you choose?

Theæt. 'Tis a perplexing choice that you set before me, Socrates.

Soc. But it certainly seems that the argument will not   D
admit of both. However,—for we are bound to make every venture,—what say you if we try to put a brazen face on the matter?

Theæt. How?

Soc. By consenting to state what we mean by 'the knowing a thing'

Theæt. Why, surely there is nothing impudent in that!

Soc. You don't seem to perceive that our whole argument from the very first has been an inquiry about knowledge We professed not to understand the meaning of the term.

Theæt. Nay, I am aware of that.

Soc. Don't you think then that it shows rather a want of modesty, while we don't understand what knowledge is, to undertake to give an opinion as to the nature and meaning of 'to know?' The fact is, Theætetus, we have long been muddled by this unclear kind of talk.[1] We have said a count-   E
less number of times 'We know,' and 'We don't know,' 'We are sure,' and 'We are not sure,' as if we could understand a word that passes between us while we remain ignorant what knowledge is[2]! Nay, at this very moment we are using the terms 'ignorant' and 'understand,' as if we had any right in the world[3] to use them if, as we say, we are as yet destitute of knowledge.

Theæt. Then in what way do you propose to converse about these subjects, Socrates, if you avoid the use of such terms?

[1] Viz. from want of clear definitions and the true method of dialectic Literally, 'we have dirtied our mouths with arguing unclearly'

[2] "How can we use the name even in inquiry without knowing the meaning of the name?"—*Campbell*

[3] For ὡς προσῆκον we should perhaps read οὐ προσῆκον, as H Stephens proposed.

Soc. In no way at all, so long as I am what I am; though perhaps I might have done without them if I had been a practised controversialist. If such an one were now here, he 197 would say, ' Don't use the terms at all'; and he would blame us greatly for saying what I say, that we cannot possibly do without them. Well, then, since we are but poor disputants, would you approve of my making a venture, and stating what we mean by ' to know'? For it seems to me that it will serve our purpose to do so.

Theæt. Make the venture by all means; and if you don't altogether do without the words, I shall make great allowance for you.[1]

XXXVI. *Soc* Have you heard then what they now-a-days say is the meaning of ' to know'?

Theæt. I may have heard, but I don't at present remember.

Soc. If I mistake not, they say it is ' the state or condition B of having knowledge.[2]'

Theæt. True.

Soc. Let us then make a trifling change in the definition, and call it the *possession* of knowledge.

Theæt. In what respect will you maintain that the one differs from the other?[3]

Soc. Perhaps it will be found not to differ at all; however, you shall hear, and then join me in seeing if there is any truth in their apparent difference.

Theæt. I will, if I can.

Soc. Then, as it seems to me, the possessing a thing is not the same as the having it; just as a man may have bought a mantle, and have it in his possession, though he does not happen to wear it. We should not then say that he *had* it, but only that he *possessed* it.

---

[1] *i. e.* if you now and then inadvertently say 'know' or 'don't know' in discussing what 'to know' means.

[2] The earliest example, perhaps, of ἕξις in the sense of 'habit'.

[3] A man may have learnt something, but not have it ready in his memory at the moment he wants it. He then has the κτῆσις but not the ἕξις. See inf. p. 198. D.

Theæt. And rightly so.

Soc. Consider then if it is possible in the same way for C
a man to possess knowledge without actually having it. Take
the case of a person who has caught some wild birds, rock-
pigeons or any other kind, and builds a dove-cot for them, and
so keeps them at home. In one sense, no doubt, we should
say that he *has* them always, because he has secured the
possession of them.

Theæt. Yes.

Soc. But in another sense we should say he *has* not any
one of them; only that he has a present power over them,
since he has made them his captives and keeps them in a cage
of his own. He can take and hold them whenever he wishes, D
by catching whichever of them he may please at any time, and
let them go again. And this he can do as many times as ever
he may choose.

Theæt. All this is quite possible.

Soc. Now then, as before we constructed in our souls some
sort of waxen apparatus, let us again build in each soul a kind
of dove-cot for birds of every species,[1] some of them gregarious,
and keeping aloof from the rest, others that consort in small
numbers, some that fly by themselves through all the others,
this way or that as it may happen.

Theæt. Well, supposing our dove-cot made, what next? E

Soc. We must say that while we are children this receptacle
is empty; and instead of birds we must conceive that different
kinds of knowledge are meant. Whatever piece of knowledge
any one has acquired and shut up in his enclosure, we must say
of it, that he has learnt, or has found out, the fact or subject
of which this is the knowledge; and that this is 'to know.'

Theæt. Let that be granted.

Soc. Now consider what terms are required to express the
endeavour to catch a second time whatever of these kinds of
knowledge he may wish, and the taking and holding, and the 198

---

[1] *i e.* notions and ideas of various kinds, some general, some special, etc.

letting it go again.   Are they the same terms as we used
before, when he was acquiring them, or different? But perhaps
you will learn more clearly what I mean from the following
example.   Arithmetic, I suppose, you call a science?

Theæt. I do.

Soc. Conceive then this to be 'the pursuit of certain kinds
of knowledge about odd and even numbers generally.'

Theæt. I will suppose that.

Soc. It is by this science then, I suppose, that both he
himself has the different branches of knowledge of numbers in
his service and possession,[1] and in the capacity of teacher com-   B
municates them to another?

Theæt. It is so.

Soc. As then we call such a person 'a teacher', so we say
that he who receives his instruction is 'a learner'; but when
he has got it safe and fast in that dove-cot of his, by possession,
then we say that 'he knows it.'

Theæt. Certainly.

Soc. Now attend to what follows next. If a man is a
perfect master of arithmetic, he knows *all* numbers, does he
not? For he has in his soul the kinds of knowledge that
comprise them all.

Theæt. Of course.

Soc. May not such a person then sometimes make a com-   C
putation, either with himself abstractedly, or of some external
objects that are capable of being counted?[2]

Theæt. Undoubtedly.

Soc. And this 'counting up' we shall set down as nothing
more than 'considering what the sum total is.'

Theæt. Just so.

Soc. Then it comes to this: it appears that he is considering what he already knows, as if he did not know it, although

----

[1] *Under* his hand, though not perhaps *in* his hand at any given moment

[2] Reading αὐτὸ ἢ ἄλλο τι τῶν ἔξω, where αὐτὸ means 'in the abstract.'
The MSS. mostly give αὐτὰ, which may bear the same sense, but is less gram-
matical.

we allowed that he did know number generally. I suppose
you hear questions of this kind sometimes raised?

Theæt. I do.

XXXVII. *Soc.* Then we, keeping up our simile of the   D
getting our rock-pigeons, and trying to catch them, shall say,
that this catching is of two kinds, the one before one possessed
them, and with a view to possessing; the other after possessing
them, and with a view of taking and holding in the hands
what one had some time ago acquired. Just so, after a man
has long gained certain branches of sciences by learning, and
so has a knowledge of them, he may again learn up the very
same subjects by taking up the particular science of each and
getting hold of it: for, though he had long ago acquired it, he
did not happen to have it at his fingers' ends just when he
wanted it.

Theæt. True.

Soc. This, then, is the point of my late question, *how* we   E
are to use our store of terms in speaking of these subjects,—
that is, when some one skilled in arithmetic proceeds to count,
or one acquainted with letters to read. For it seems that
on such an occasion he goes to learn again from himself what
he already knows!

Theæt. That sounds odd, Socrates.

Soc. Well, are we to say that he is going to read or to
count what he does *not* know, when we have already granted
him the science of all letters and all number?   199

Theæt. Why, that too would be unreasonable.

Soc. Do you prefer then that we should say, that we care
nothing about terms, or how any one likes to drag this way or
that 'knowledge' and 'learning', but that, as we have distin-
quished *possessing* knowledge from *having* it, we should affirm[1]
it is impossible not to possess[2] what one possesses? For thus
it can never happen that a man does not know what he knows,
though he may conceive a false opinion respecting it. For

---

[1] Reading φῶμεν for φαμέν.
[2] Using κεκτῆσθαι in place of ἔχειν.

it is possible for him not to have at hand the *particular* know-   B
ledge of the subject, but some other knowledge instead of it.
And this may happen whenever, in chasing some one of the
bits of knowledge that keep flying away from him,[1] he gets
hold of one by mistake instead of the other; as when he
fancied the sum of eleven was twelve, and so got hold of his
knowledge of eleven instead of his knowledge of twelve,—his
ringdove, as it were, instead of his rock-pigeon.

Theæt. That certainly seems reasonable.

Soc. But when he has captured the particular one which
he wants to take, then we shall say that he is not mistaken,
but has a true opinion. Under these circumstances there may
· be both true and false opinion, and none of our former diffi-   C
culties any longer stand in our way. Perhaps now you will
agree with me in this: or what course do you propose to take?

Theæt. I agree.

Soc. For we have thus got rid of that 'not knowing what
people know', for it no longer comes to this, in any part of our
argument, that we don't possess what we do possess,[2] either
when we are deceived in something or when we are not.—But
there is another still more formidable difficulty looming in the
distance, of which I seem to get a glimpse.[3]

Theæt. What is that?

Soc. The possibility that the changing one piece of
knowledge for another may sometimes constitute 'false opinion'.

Theæt. How so?

Soc. The difficulty consists first in a man's having a   D
knowledge of something and yet being ignorant of it, not
from want of knowledge, but from the very fact of his own

---

[1] Construe ἀπ' αὐτοῦ διαπετομένων. Mr. Campbell refers ἀπ' αὐτοῦ to
ὃ κέκτηται, "some particular knowledge from his stock." Perhaps we should
read ἐπιστημῶν.

[2] Since we can distinguish between ἔχειν and κεκτῆσθαι. So 'not knowing'
may mean 'not having in one's memory at the moment.'

[3] Or, 'I seem to get a glimpse of something more serious that may befal our
argument', i. e. worse defeat than before.

knowledge.[1] Secondly, to think A is B or B is A, is surely
something that we can hardly account for. For here we have
knowledge present in the soul, and yet the soul knows nothing,
but is ignorant of everything! Why, according to this argument, nothing prevents the very presence of ignorance causing
us to know, or blindness making a man see, if, as we say,
knowledge can ever make one ignorant.

Theæt. Perhaps, Socrates, we were wrong in making our   E
birds only to represent the various kinds of knowledge. We
ought to have assumed that there are also divers kinds of
unscientific notions flying about with them in the soul; and
thus when one gives chase and catches at one time a knowledge, at another a non-knowledge on the same subject, he has
a false opinion by the unscientific, a true one by the scientific
conception.

Soc. One can hardly abstain from praising you, Theætetus.
But consider again what you have just said. We will take your
view of the matter: the person, you say, who gets hold of 200
the unscientific notion will have a false opinion. Is it not so?

Theæt. Yes.

Soc. Of course, he will not also think that he has a false
opinion?

Theæt. That is not likely.

Soc. But a true one: he will consider himself in the
position of one who knows, in the very matter about which he
is in error.

Theæt. Of course.

Soc. He will think, therefore, that he has caught and
holds a knowledge and not a non-knowledge?

Theæt. Evidently.

---

[1] Since he changes or confounds two things which he knows. His catching the wrong bird, as it were, is due to his having also the right one in the
cage, i. e. there could be no wrong one unless there was also a right one. From
this ensues the real or apparent paradox, that a man may be ignorant through
knowledge. Compare the statement in *Phaed.* p. 68. D, that men may be brave
through cowardice and temperate through licentiousness.

Soc. Then, after this long round-about, here we find ourselves again at our original difficulty. For our captious friend
will say, with a smile at our simplicity, 'Tell me, my good   B
friends, do you mean that a man who knows both science and
want of science, thinks that one which he knows is some other
of what he knows[1]; or, knowing neither of them, does he come
to the conclusion that one which he does not know is another
of what he does not know[2], or, knowing one but not the other,
does he think the one he knows is the one he does not know,
or conversely, the one he does not know is the one he knows?
Or will you tell me that even of the sciences and non-sciences,
there are again and in turn other sciences,[3] the possessor of
which shuts them up in some other absurd dove-cots or houses
built of wax, and thus, so long as he possesses them, *knows*   C
them, even if he has not got them in his soul ready to hand?
Will you thus (he will add) be compelled to go round and
round a countless number of times, and make no progress at
all?' What shall we reply to this, Theætetus?

Theæt. Upon my word, Socrates, I don't know what we
are to say.

Soc. Does not the argument then justly find fault with
us, and warn us that we are wrong in looking for false opinion
before we have found knowledge, and in dismissing that?
Whereas it is impossible to understand the former, till one has   D
got a sufficiently clear conception of what exact knowledge is.

Theæt. At present, Socrates, we are compelled to think as
you say.

XXXVIII. *Soc.* Then let us begin again once more,
and see what definition of knowledge any of us will give. For
I suppose we shall not give it up yet.

Theæt. Certainly not, unless indeed you are getting tired
of it.

---

[1] Which was ἀδύνατον, sup. p. 192. A. He cannot mistake ignorance of a
subject for knowledge of it.

[2] ὃ μὴ οἶδεν, ὃ μὴ οἶδεν αὖ. *Ibid.*

[3] That the very fact of distinguishing the knowledge from the non-knowledge of a subject is a science.

Soc. Say then what we had best call it so as least to contradict ourselves.

Theæt. What we before proposed to call it, Socrates, for E I myself have no other name to give it.

Soc. What is that?

Theæt. We will say that 'true opinion' constitutes knowledge. Surely there can be no error in holding right opinions, and all the actions proceeding from it must be sound and right.

Soc. 'The result will show,' Theætetus, as the man said who was the first to cross the river.[1] Just so, if we keep sounding this question as we advance, perhaps, by presenting some obstacle to our progress, it will of itself show us what we 201 are looking for[2], whereas if we stand still nothing will become clear to us.

Theæt. You say well: let us proceed and keep a good look out ahead.

Soc. Well, this at least will require no long consideration: there is one whole branch[3] of art that shows you that true opinion is not knowledge.

Theæt. How so? What art do you mean?

Soc. That of those distinguished professors of wisdom, your orators and your 'men of law', as they are called. Surely they, in the exercise of their art, persuade people not so much by teaching and informing, as by making them think whatever they choose to tell them. Supposing some persons were robbed of their money, or violently treated in some other way, and no witnesses were by; do you imagine there are any teachers in B the world so clever as to be able to inform the jury, in a

[1] When there was a doubt whether it was fordable.

[2] *i. e.* it will at least show that ἐπιστήμη is not ἀληθὴς δόξα. Like a sudden increase of depth in the ford, a difficulty will arise to stop us. Stallbaum misses the sense in translating "etiamsi nobis fuerit impedimento." Mr. Campbell takes ἐμπόδιον in a different sense, 'by letting us touch the bottom with our feet.'

[3] The words ὅλη τέχνη should rather mean 'all art', *i.e.* art in general. But this sense is inconsistent with the context, unless τέχνη can *specially* mean ῥητορική.

limited space of time, of the exact truth of what happened to them?[1]

Theæt. I don't think they could *prove* it to them; but still they might convince them.

Soc. By 'convincing' you mean 'causing them to think', I suppose?

Theæt. Of course.

Soc. Then when the jury are rightly and truly convinced about circumstances which only he who saw them can *know* to be facts, and no one else; then, deciding about them on hear-   C
say, and by the right conviction they have got, they may be said to decide without knowledge[2], but because they have been led to take a correct view of the case,—that is, if their verdict is right.

Theæt. Certainly that is so.

Soc. But surely, my friend, if true opinion and knowledge[3] were really identical, no juryman, however shrewd, would form a right conclusion without knowledge. But it now appears that one of these is different from the other.

Theæt. Yes, Socrates, that is just what I once heard some one say, but had forgotten it, though now I think of it. He contended that only the true opinion which was able to give a reason for it, was knowledge, but that which could not   D
give an account of itself was not to be classed with 'knowledge' at all. Thus, things of which you can give no account are 'unknowable' (so he called them), but if you can, they are 'knowable.'

Soc. Really, you give a very good definition. How then

---

[1] Reading τούτοις with good MSS, including the Bodleian, (according to Mr. Campbell). The argument from εἰκότα, probabilities rather than from facts, πράγματα, is here alluded to, and more fully illustrated in *Phædr.* p. 273. B. "In the case of judicial evidence, a true opinion may be formed by the judges without the possibility of knowledge, since in questions of fact nothing short of personal observation ensures certainty."—*Mr. Campbell.*

[2] If that means the αἴσθησις of actual sight.

[3] The words καὶ δικαστήρια may have come from a marginal gloss κατὰ δικαστήρια in the sense of ἐν δικαστηρίοις.

did he distinguish what we can from what we cannot know[1]?
Tell me, for I should like to learn if you and I have been
taught the same.

Theæt. I am not sure that I can make it out[2], though
perhaps, if another were to say it, I might follow.

XXXIX. *Soc.* Then hear a dream of mine as a set-off
to yours.[3] For I, on the other hand, fancy I heard some
persons say, that the first principles, or elements as we may   E
call them,[4] from which we and all visible things are composed,
have no account that can be given of them; we can only give
each of them a name as an abstraction, but we can predicate
nothing else about them, not even Being or non-Being. For if
so, there is added to it existence or non-existence; whereas we
ought to apply no qualities, if one is to speak of a simple element.[5]   202
Nay, we must not add even 'itself,' or 'that', nor 'each,' nor
'only,' nor 'this,' nor many other attributes of the like kind.[6]
For these terms are applied to all things in a perpetual round,
and are in themselves different from the things to which they
are applied; but, if a thing can be spoken of *per se*[7], and
a proper account can be given of it, it ought to be described
without any of these accessories. But, as the case really
stands, it is impossible that any of the first principles should

---

[1] *i. e* how did he expound this μετὰ λόγου?

[2] He had said above ἐπιλελήσμην.

[3] For ἀκούσας ἐπιλελήσμην virtually means ἐδόκουν ἀκούειν. The 'dream'
of Socrates here is probably the doctrine of Heraclitus, though the 'Being' and
'not Being' is a doctrine of the Eleatics, discussed at length in the *Sophistes*.

[4] The words οἱονπερεὶ στοιχεῖα read like a grammarian's gloss.

[5] See *Sophist.* p. 239.

[6] Sc. ἃ ἂν ἱστῇ τῷ λόγῳ, which give a distinct and concrete existence, and
by which things cease to be abstractions, or, in other words, *notions* become
things. The words οὐδὲ τοῦτο may have come from a marginal correction of
οὐδὲ τὸ αὐτό.

[7] With deference to Mr. Campbell, it may be urged that αὐτὸ is necessarily
emphatic, being in the nominative. The meaning is, that if a thing is capable
of being named by a term that conveys a definite idea of it, no further description or particularising is required.

be described in terms, since it can only be *named* at the most.[1] ` B
But when we come to consider compounds of them, then as
they are themselves combined, so the terms used to describe
them are combined so as to become an account or definition of
them. For the combination of terms is the very essence of
a definition. Thus then the primary elements are undefinable
and unknowable, and are merely objects of sensation; but the
combinations are knowable and definable and comprehensible
by a true and correct view. When then a person has got the
true conception of anything without being able to give an
account of it, we say that his soul holds the truth about it,
though he cannot be said to *know* it. For one who can neither   C
give nor get an account of a thing, is without any scientific
knowledge about that particular thing. But when he has got
the further power of defining it, he has become able in *all*
these respects[2], and is perfect in wisdom. Was this the
purport of the dream *you* heard, or was it different?[3]

Theæt. Nay, it was quite as you describe it.

Soc. Then do you accept this view, and put it thus:
'Knowledge is right opinion where you can give a reason
for it'?

Theæt. Precisely so.

Soc. May we not say, then, Theætetus, that we have thus   D
at last, on this very day, got hold of that which in times past
many philosophers have been seeking for, but have grown old
before they could find it?

Theæt. To me at all events, Socrates, the definition we
have now arrived at appears to be a sound one.

---

[1] In an unscientific age, 'fire' or 'air' could only be *named* as elements. Of
their qualities, origin, and nature, absolutely nothing was known. Even to
modern chemistry some bodies, like gold, are simple, and cannot be analysed, or
their existence explained. If, however, we speak of "jeweller's gold," we can
give an account of it (λόγον ἔχει). We say it is an alloy made up of certain
proportions of gold and silver and copper.

[2] δοῦναι καὶ δέξασθαι λόγον, γιγώσκειν, ἐπιστήμονα εἶναι, ἀληθεύειν περὶ
αὐτό.

[3] Sup. D, λέγε εἰ ἄρα κατὰ ταῦτα σύ τε κἀγὼ ἀκηκόαμεν.

Soc. Why, probability is in favour of its being just what we have said.[1] For, apart from right opinion and a rational account of it, what have we left that we can fairly call knowledge? There is one point, however, in our definition that I cannot quite accept.

Theæt. Well, what is that!

Soc. The proposition that seems[2] to be very neatly and cleverly stated, ' The primaries are unknowable, but all that comes under the head of *combinations* may be known.'

Theæt. Was not that rightly said?   E

Soc. We will inquire; for we hold as it were hostages for the argument[3] in the examples which our instructor made use of when he told us all this.

Theæt. What examples do you mean?

Soc. The single letters and their combinations in the alphabet. You don't suppose that, in making these remarks, the speaker had anything else in view?[4]

Theæt. No, I think he referred to them.

XL. *Soc.* Then let us take up these examples and put 203 them to a severe test,—or rather, let us apply such a test to ourselves, and see whether we learnt our letters on this principle or otherwise. And let me ask first:—is it not the case, that the combinations have a meaning, while the mere letters are meaningless?

Theæt. Perhaps it is.

Soc. I quite think so, too. For instance, take the name

---

[1] "The definition itself, whatever may be said of the theory."—*Mr. Campbell.* It seems not improbable that either αὐτὸ or τοῦτο is a gloss or a variety of reading.

[2] Perhaps ἐδόκει should be read for δοκεῖ.

[3] For the truth or fallacy of it, like the keeping or breaking of a treaty. The *hostages* being put to the *torture* mean the examples put to the test.

[4] Lit. ' or do you think the speaker spoke what we now say (viz. about στοιχεῖα being ἄγνωστα, etc.) with a view to any other things than to the alphabet?' *i. e.* don't you think he had the alphabet specially in view? The illustration (of synthesis and analysis) from letters is given somewhat fully in *Philebus*, p. 17, and *Republ.* p. 277, seq.

Socrates, and suppose some one to put the question in this way, 'Theætetus, what is $\Sigma\Omega$?' what answer will you give?

Theæt. That it is Σ and Ω.

Soc. Then that is the account which you have to give of the syllable?

Theæt. It is.

Soc. Now then give me the like account of the Σ.   B

Theæt. Of course one can't tell the elements that make an element! You know, Socrates, that Σ is one of the consonants, —a mere sound, a sort of hissing, produced by the tongue. But B is a mute, and has no sound of its own at all, like the majority of the letters. So that they are quite rightly called *meaningless*, when the most distinct of them, the seven vowels, have only vocal sound, but no power of expression whatever.[1]

Soc. So far then, my friend, we have set on a right footing the question about knowledge.

Theæt. We seem to have done so.

Soc. Well, but wait. Are we sure we have correctly stated our opinion that only the syllable, but not the letter, is   C the subject of knowledge?

Theæt. There is little doubt of that.

Soc. Tell me now; do we mean by this word *syllable* both letters, (or all of them, if there be more than two,) or some one general form of language[2] produced by the combination of them?

Theæt. All the letters together, I should say.

Soc. Consider now in the case of two, Σ and Ω. Together they form the first syllable of my name. Does not one who knows it know both letters?

Theæt. Of course.   D

Soc. Then he does know the Σ and the Ω.[3]

Theæt. Yes.

[1] A sort of play on the senses, 'they have only a voice, but no *talk*,' and 'they have only articulate sound, but no account can be given of them.'

[2] Or, 'kind of articulate sound.'

[3] If he knows $\Sigma\Omega$ combined, he must know $\Sigma+\Omega$.

Soc. Do you mean to say then that he is ignorant of each separately, and while he knows neither yet he knows both?

Theæt. Why that, Socrates, would be strange and unreasonable indeed.

Soc. But surely, as one must needs know each, if he is to know both, it is quite inevitable that he must know the letters first, if he is ever to know the combination at all. And thus that clever proposition of ours[1] will run off and leave us in the lurch.

Theæt. And very suddenly too.   E

Soc. The fact is, we don't keep a good guard over it.[2] We ought perhaps to have defined the syllable not to be composed of the letters merely, but as a sort of vocal sound produced from them, having a special character of its own,[3] that of the letters themselves being distinct.

Theæt. I quite think so. Perhaps the matter stands thus rather than as we said before.

Soc. We must consider it well, and not give up in such a cowardly way an important and serious discussion.[4]

Theæt. No, indeed.

Soc. Then let us take for granted that a syllable[5] is, as we 204 now say, a class of its own peculiar kind resulting from the union of the several composing elements; and let us assume this not only of letters, but of all combinations without any exception.

Theæt. Certainly.

Soc. Then there ought not to be *parts* in it.

Theæt. Why?

Soc. Because, if anything has parts, the whole must of necessity be made up of *all* the parts. Or do you venture

---

[1] About ἄγνωστα στοιχεῖα.

[2] As over a runaway slave.

[3] We might say, and with truth, that SO was not merely S combined with O, but 'a certain intonation of voice composed of sibilant and palatal.'

[4] Lit. 'a great and a fine topic.'

[5] Or 'the complex', in a general sense, a 'one indivisible nature', inf.

to say that a whole made up of parts has a nature of its own different from all the parts ?[1]

Theæt. I do.

Soc. Do you call then ' all' the same as ' whole', or do you think each is different ?[2]   B

Theæt. I have no clear answer to give, but as you tell me to answer promptly, I say at a venture that it is different.

Soc. Your readiness, Theætetus, is right; whether your answer also is, we have to consider.

Theæt. Certainly we have.

XLI. *Soc.* Then, according to our present statement, the whole will be something different from *all* of a thing.

Theæt. Yes.

Soc. Well now, do all the ciphers of a sum differ from the sum total ? For instance, when we count separately, one, two, three, four, five, six, and when we say twice three, or three   C times two, or $4 + 2$, or $3 + 2 + 1$, or $5 + 1$, do we in all these forms of expression say the same or something different ?

Theæt. The same.

Soc. And that is nothing more nor less than six ?

Theæt. Nothing else.

Soc. In each expression then we mention the whole number six ?

Theæt. Yes.

Soc. But surely in naming *all* the ciphers we specify the total amount ?[3]

Theæt. That must be so.

Soc. That is to say, six ?

Theæt. We mean nothing else.

Soc. Then, in numeration at least, we mean the very same   D thing by ' all' and ' all the ciphers together.'

---

[1] A whole (uncut) apple has a character distinct from the two halves, or four quarters, into which another apple has been cut.

[2] That to be whole is one thing, and to contain all the parts is another.

[3] *i e.* when we say πάντα τὰ ἑξ we mean that ἑξ is πᾶν, or includes every component cipher. I have ventured to read πᾶν in place of πάλιν, from which I can extract no meaning.

Theæt. It seems so.

Soc. Then our expression amounts to this, that the number of square feet in a plethrum is the same as a plethrum? Is it not?

Theæt. Yes.

Soc. And so the number of feet in a stadium?

Theæt. Yes.

Soc. And, of course, the number of men in a camp, means the same as the camp, and so on with all other things of the like kind. For the whole number is the existing aggregate in each case.[1]

Theæt. That is so.

Soc. But the number contained in each thing constitutes its *parts*, does it not?

Theæt. It does.   E

Soc. And all things which have parts are made up of parts?

Theæt. I should say so.

Soc. And it is admitted that all the parts form the total, if the whole number makes the total?[2]

Theæt. It is so.

Soc. Then 'the whole' is not made up of parts; for it would be the sum total, if it were all the parts.[3]

Theæt. It seems not

Soc. Now, is 'a part' a part of anything else than of the whole?

Theæt. Yes, of the sum total.

Soc. You fight like a man, Theætetus. And is not 'the sum total' that which we call it, when no part is absent?   205

Theæt. Of course.

---

[1] *i. e.* there is no other πᾶν than what is made by ὁ πᾶς ἀριθμός.

[2] Since the ἀριθμὸς is the μέρη.

[3] Theætetus had ventured the assertion that πᾶν was different from ὅλον, sup. B. If therefore πᾶν is made up of all the parts, ὅλον can not be. In a sense, this is obviously true: the four quarters of an apple are not a whole (uncut) apple, though no part is wanting.

Soc. And is not 'the whole' the very same thing,—that is to say, from which no part anywhere is removed? For whenever part is wanting, a thing is neither a whole nor 'all there', —if the same result follows at the same time from the same deficiency.

Theæt. It appears to me now that 'all' and whole do not differ.

Soc. Well, now, we said, I think,[1] that if a thing has parts, *all* these parts will constitute the whole and the sum total

Theæt. Yes, to be sure.

Soc. Again then let me ask, in reference to the point I was endeavouring to prove, Is it not a necessary consequence   B that, if the syllable is not the letters,[2] it does not contain the letters as the parts of it; or, if it *is* the same as its parts, then it is equally with them a subject of knowledge?

Theæt. It is so.

Soc. It was to avoid this conclusion then that we assumed the syllable was different from its parts.[3]

Theæt. Just so.

Soc. Well, but if the *letters* are not parts of the syllable, can you tell us any other things that are parts of a syllable without being letters of it?[4]

Theæt. I cannot: for if, Socrates, I were to grant that a syllable had parts,[5] it would be absurd to give up the letters and go in quest of something else.

Soc. Then according to the present argument, Theætetus,   C a syllable will decidedly prove to be one indivisible nature.

Theæt. So it seems.

Soc. Do you remember then, my friend, that a little while

---

[1] p. 204 A, οὗ ἂν ᾖ μέρη, τὸ ὅλον ἀνάγκη τὰ πάντα μέρη εἶναι.

[2] Or, in a larger sense, 'if the compound thing is not the component elements.' Cf p 203 E, χρὴ γὰρ ἴσως τὴν συλλαβὴν τίθεσθαι μὴ τὰ στοιχεῖα.

[3] A μία τις ἰδέα, *i. e.* something having a distinct character of its own.

[4] *i e* if the *letters* are not μέρη, what are?

[5] *i. e.* and was not μία τις ἰδέα.

ago[1] we accepted the proposition, and thought that it was well put, ' We cannot tell what the primaries are from which compound bodies are made.' For each primary is itself uncompounded, and it would not be correct to predicate of it either ' Being'[2] or any special quality or condition, since these are different[3] from and alien to it; and this[4] is the cause which makes it both beyond reason and incapable of being known.

Theæt. I remember.

Soc. Is not then this, and none but this, the cause of its being uniform and indivisible? For myself, I can see no other.[5]   D

Theæt. No, indeed, I think there is not.

Soc. Does not then the syllable we have been speaking of fall into the same class as the other, if it has no parts, and is one nature?

Theæt. Decidedly so.

Soc. Then if the syllable is an aggregate of several letters and a whole, and its component parts are letters, the syllables must be equally capable of being known and defined as the letters themselves are, since it has been shown that all the parts are the same as the whole.

Theæt. Certainly.   E

Soc. But if it is one and without parts, then both the syllable and the primary element are alike indescribable and unintelligible, as the same cause will make them so.

Theæt. I cannot state the case in any other way.

Soc. Then don't let us listen to anyone who says that a syllable may be known and defined, but a letter is something of a contrary kind.[6]

---

[1] p. 201. E.

[2] For that would be adding a known attribute to an unknown thing.

[3] As being γνωστά.

[4] Viz. the impossibility of giving any account or definition of τὰ πρῶτα.

[5] We cannot be said to *know* a thing of which we can give no account; and that of which we can give no account cannot be analyzed, but must be taken as one homogeneous and uniform body. We can only say that gold is gold, though we can say that bronze is copper and tin in certain proportions.

[6] For both are either one or the other, knowable or unknowable.

Theæt. No indeed, if we are to follow our argument.

Soc. And now let us ask again,[1]—would you not rather 206 accept the statement to the contrary, from what you know of your own experience in learning letters?

Theæt. What do you mean?

Soc. That you went on for a long time learning nothing else but only trying to distinguish at sight and by the ear each and every letter by itself, that you might not be puzzled by the position of them in spoken or written language.

Theæt. That is very true.

Soc. Well, did not complete instruction from your music-master consist solely in your being able to follow each tone, B and knowing to what note it belonged? Everyone will allow that this is what we meant by 'the elements of music.'

Theæt. Nothing but that.

Soc. If then we are entitled to make inferences from elements and combinations familiar to ourselves in reference to others, we shall contend that the class of primaries in general is capable of being much more clearly known, and the knowledge of them has far greater influence, than the combinations have, in acquiring perfectly each kind of knowledge. So, if anyone says that the combination may be known, but the element by its very nature cannot be known, we shall think that he is joking, either on purpose or without intending it.

Theæt. Quite so.

XLII. *Soc* Well, this is a point[2] on which further C proofs may yet appear, as it seems to me. But let us not forget, through attending to it, to see and understand what we mean by the proposition, 'The most perfect knowledge is Right Opinion where you can also give a reason for it.'

Theæt. Then it is our duty to look into it.

Soc. Tell me then, what is the meaning of this phrase,

---

[1] Or, 'But what of the other view?'

[2] Viz the question if the syllable may be known while the elements (letters) are unknown.

'*Reason* shows us?'[1] For to me it appears to say one of three things.

Theæt. What are they?

Soc The first perhaps is, the making one's meaning D plain by the means of voice with phrases and words, and so as it were taking an impression of it on the current proceeding from the mouth, as if one were catching a reflection on a mirror or on the surface of water.[2] Does it not appear to you that the word λόγος is something of this sort?

Theæt. To me it seems so. For instance, we say that he who does this 'speaks'.

Soc There is one thing then that any one can do more or less quickly,—I mean the *explaining* his views on any matter, unless he is deaf or dumb from his birth. And thus all who E have a right opinion will be seen to have it together with the power of expressing it; and right opinion will no longer occur apart and distinct from knowledge.

Theæt. True.

Soc. Then don't let us rashly condemn a man for talking nonsense who may have given his opinion[3] that knowledge is that which we are now considering.[4] For perhaps, when some one said so, he did not mean exactly this, but 'the being able, when one is asked what something is, to give one's reply to the question by dealing with the primaries.'[5] 207

Theæt. Give an example of what you mean, Socrates.

Soc. We will take what Hesiod says about a waggon, that

---

[1] We should read, I think, τί ποτε βούλεται τὸ τὸν λόγον ἡμῖν σημαίνειν.

[2] *i. e.* an evanescent, intangible impress. The first meaning then is 'a kind of mental talk.'

[3] τὸν ἀποφηνάμενον, the subject to εἰρηκέναι, should rather have been the genitive after καταγιγνώσκωμεν. The idiom is familiar in καταγιγνώσκειν μωρίαν or θάνατόν τινος.

[4] Viz. ὀρθὴ δόξα μετὰ λόγου.

[5] To give an account of it by stating what the elements are which compose it, and not by a mere description of its form or qualities. See sup. p. 147 A, seqq.

it contains 'a hundred pieces of wood.' Now, *I* could not specify them, nor, I dare say, could you. We should be quite content, if we were asked 'What is a waggon?' to be able to reply, 'Wheels, axle, body, upper rail, yoke'.[1]

Theæt. Certainly.

Soc. But he, perhaps, would think we were making fools of ourselves,—just as if we were asked your name, and gave it in syllables as The-æe-te-tus. He might say, 'You both think   B and speak rightly in giving this reply, but it is absurd in you to suppose that you are learned in language, and that your account of Theætetus' name is given as if you grammatically understood it.' No! he would say it was impossible to define anything scientifically, unless a man goes into each matter thoroughly, not only having a right opinion about it, but taking into account all the component elements, as we said before.

Theæt. That was what we stated.

Soc. In the same way, then, he will think that though we had a correct notion about a waggon, yet that one who could describe its real nature by enumerating all the hundred planks,   C and had gained that further knowledge respecting it, had acquired the power of giving an account of it over and above the right notion of it; and thus had become a man of art and science in place of a man of mere opinion respecting the mechanism of a waggon, since he could describe it as a whole by specifying its component parts.

Theæt. And do you think, Socrates, all this is rightly said?

Soc. If *you* think so, my friend, and if you accept the method of inquiry by primary parts as the true explanation of everything,[2] but that by groups, or general combinations of a still more general kind, as an irrational procedure,—say so, that we may further consider it.

---

[1] He omits the pole, ῥυμὸς, to the end of which the yoke is fastened.

[2] Lit. 'the going through the (constituent) elements as the true way to give an account of each (compound).' It is hard to say whether περὶ ἕκαστον should be construed with διέξοδον or with λόγον.

Theæt. Yes, I fully accept it   D

Soc. And do you think that anyone *knows* any subject when he fancies the same element belongs at one time to the same, at another to another thing; or when also he imagines that now one, now another, belongs to the same thing?[1]

Theæt. Upon my word, I don't think that can be so.

Soc. Have you forgotten then that in the learning of your letters at first both you and your other schoolfellows did this very thing?

Theæt. You mean, don't you, that we thought[2] first one letter, then another, belonged to the same syllable; and that   E we put the same letter now into the proper syllable, now into some other?

Soc. That is what I mean.

Theæt. Then certainly I don't forget that; and I think persons in such a mental condition cannot be said as yet to understand.

Soc. What then? When, in such a case, a person wanting to write the name 'Theætetus' thinks he ought to write, and actually does write, Θ and E, or, intending to write 'Theo-   208 dorus', thinks he ought to use and does use T and E, shall we say that he has any real knowledge of the first syllable of your names?

Theæt. We admitted just now that a person with such notions as that was as yet ignorant.

Soc And is there any reason why the same person should not make similar mistakes about the second, third, and fourth syllables?

[1] Can a man know anything by its elements when he refers those elements to wrong combinations, *e.g* (1) when he thinks that a wheel belongs at one time to a waggon, at another to a table, or, (2) when he thinks a waggon sometimes has wheels, sometimes legs.

[2] We thought that Socrates was spelt first with a Σ and then with a Ψ, and (2) that Σ belonged first to Σωκράτης and then to ψυχή The illustrations, it will be observed, invert the order of the propositions just above. Both are cases of misconceptions respecting πρῶτα or στοιχεῖα, and both make any real knowledge of the συλλαβή impossible.

K

Theæt   None at all.

Soc.   Of course then, as now possessing the way of getting through the word by means of its component parts, he will write 'Theætetus' with a correct opinion about it, when he writes the letters and syllables consecutively.

Theæt   Clearly so.

Soc.   But at present without a scientific knowledge, but   B *only* a correct opinion, as we affirm?

Theæt   Yes.

Soc.   And yet he has *reason* for what he does besides his correct opinion.   For he knew the way of writing by syllables when he wrote it: and that, you are aware, we called the reasonable account of it.

Theæt.   True.

Soc.   It seems then, my friend, that there is a right opinion with a reasonable account, which we are not yet entitled to call 'science'.

Theæt.   So it seems.

XLIII. *Soc.*   We only dreamed then, I suppose, that we had got rich, when we imagined we were in possession of the truest account of knowledge.   Or must we not condemn it as yet?   It is just possible that some one will define knowledge not as we have done, but as the remaining notion out of three,[1]   C one of which, as we said, he who defines knowledge to be 'Right opinion with a reason for it,' must consider 'reason' to be.

Theæt   You are quite right in reminding me; there *is* one which yet remains.   One account we gave of 'the reason of an opinion' was 'the representing, as it were, of one's meaning expressed in voice'[2]; the second, which we have just discussed, was 'the progress towards the Whole through its Parts'.   And now what is the third you speak of?

Soc.   Just that which most people would tell you of,—'the

---

[1] *i. e.* λόγον ἔχειν τινὸς means σημεῖον ἔχειν εἰπεῖν, ᾧ τοῦτο τῶν ἄλλων πάντων διαφέρει, inf.

[2] P. 206. D. See *Phileb.* p. 18. C.

having some characteristic mark to appeal to, by which the thing you are asked about differs from all others'.

Theæt. What subject will you take as an example, and what account will you thus give me of it?

Soc. With respect to the sun, for instance, I suppose it is   D enough if I prove to you that it is *the* brightest of all the heavenly bodies that move round the earth.

Theæt. Certainly.

Soc. Observe now the point of the remark It is this, as we said just now : if you realize the difference by which each thing is distinguished from all others, you will realize (accord- to some) the 'true account' of a thing [1] But if you fix on some property which is common to other things, your definition will comprehend those [2] to which the common property extends.

Theæt. I understand you, and I think it is quite fair to   E call some such rule as this the 'rational account' of a thing.

Soc And whoever, beside a right opinion about any matter, has also learnt its difference from all others, will have become accurately informed on the particular subject on which before he had only an opinion

Theæt. We say this, certainly.

Soc. For myself, then, Theætetus, I can truly say that on coming close to what I shall call the outline or cartoon of our subject, I don't understand it in the least; although, while I stood some way from it, [3] there did seem to me to be something in what we said.

Theæt In what sense do you say this?

Soc. I will explain, if I can So long as I have a right   209 opinion about you, I have *only* an opinion; but if I also get an *account* of you [4], then I am said to *know* you.

---

[1] *e. g.* the best account or definition of Man is that he has reason and speech, which animals are thought not to have, or to have in a very inferior degree Whereas, if we describe Man as a biped, this definition includes some animals

[2] Or, 'will be a definition of all those', etc

[3] Eur *Ion* 585, οὐ ταὐτὸν εἶδος φαίνεται τῶν πραγμάτων πόρρωθεν ὄντων ἐγγύθεν θ' ὁρωμένων

[4] Viz. in some characteristic and distinguishing mark

Theæt. Yes.

Soc. And this 'account of you' was the way I had of expressing your difference.

Theæt. It was so.

Soc. When then I *only* had my opinion, may we not say, that I did not realise in my mind any of the marks by which you differ from the rest?

Theæt. It seems you did not. ·

Soc. Then I only had my thoughts about some of the common properties, which you do not possess in a greater degree than others.[1]

Theæt. That must be so.　　　　　　　　　　　　　　B

Soc. Then answer me, in Heaven's name! How in the world could I, in such a case, have an opinion about *you* more than about anyone else? Suppose me, for instance, to have an idea that Theætetus means ' the individual who is human, and has nose, eyes, and mouth', and so on with each of the other limbs. Is there anything in this conception which will cause me to think of Theætetus rather than of Theodore, or (as the proverb is) the lowest of the low?[2]

Theæt. Why indeed should it?

Soc. Well, if I think of you not only as the person who has a nose and eyes, but also as the one who has a turned up　　C nose and prominent eyes,[3] shall I, again, think of you more than of myself, or of others who have the like features?

Theæt. Not at all.

Soc. No; Theætetus, I suppose, will not be presented to

---

[1] " Rationem concludit in hunc modum : Si λόγος ita dicitur, ut sit definitio qua cujusque rei differentia ab alus similibus atque propriae virtutes describantur, consequens erit, ut δόξα nunquam peculiare quiddam habere, et ad universalia tantummodo pertinere existimanda sit. Quod tamen longe secus habet, siquidem etiam per δόξαν efficitur ut res singulas discernamus "—*Stallbaum.* It has already been remarked, that δόξα means 'judgment on sensation '

[2] The 'last of the Mysians' was perhaps a military proverb for a worthless ally. See on *Gorg.* p. 521 B

[3] See sup p. 143. E.

my thoughts till the peculiar curve of his nose impresses and
leaves on my mind and memory some specific difference from
all other upturned noses that I have ever seen, and so with
the other characteristics by which I shall know you,[1] and
which will remind me of you, should I meet you tomorrow,
and make me think correctly about you.

Theæt. Very true.

Soc. It seems then that correct opinion also[2] will be con-   D
cerned with the difference in each object.

Theæt Yes, so it appears.

Soc. Then what can be the meaning, after this, of 'getting
an account besides a right opinion?' For, if it means to 'get
a further opinion how one thing differs from the rest,' the
injunction to do so seems positively absurd.

Theæt. How so?

Soc. Why, it bids us get in addition a right opinion about
things, of which we already have a right opinion as to their
difference from others! And so the moving round and round
of a wooden roller, or a pestle, or anything of the sort, would   E
be nothing at all compared to such a command as that![3] It
would be more properly called an order given by a blind man;
for to tell us to get in addition what we already have, in order
to understand opinions that we form, does seem like the act of
one who is very much in the dark indeed.[4]

Theæt. Come, then,[5] tell me what was it you were just
now going to say, when you asked the question?

Soc. If, my young friend, 'the getting a true account

---

[1] The text here has some corruption. I propose to read (as I have translated), ἐξ ὧν εἴσομαί σε, καὶ ἐμὲ, ἐὰν αὔριον ἀπαντήσω, ἀναμνήσει.

[2] As well as the λόγος, the peculiar province of which was 'to differentiate'

[3] A proverb expressing the useless or endless repetition of the same act.

[4] A blind man might say, 'take your stick as well as your hat', not seeing
that you already had both

[5] The MSS. corruptly give εἴγε δή τι, etc. I have ventured to read εἶα δή,
τί νῦν ὡς ἐρῶν ἐπύθου. The question asked was, τὸ προσλαβεῖν λόγον τί ἂν ἔτι
εἴη; and Theætetus seems to have thought Socrates was himself going to define
it.

besides' means that we are *to know*, and not merely to have
an opinion about, the difference; then this, the best of all the
accounts about knowledge that have been given, will prove
rather a sorry affair; for 'to know' is 'to get exact information,'
I suppose. Is it not? 210

Theæt. Yes.

Soc. Then when we inquire of our argument, what knowledge is, it seems it will reply, 'Right opinion with knowledge
of difference.' For, according to it, this will be the 'getting
an account, over and above the mere opinion.'

Theæt. It does appear so.

Soc. And surely it is utterly weak and silly, if, when we
are inquiring what knowledge is, to give as a reply, 'Right
opinion with knowledge,'—be it 'of difference' or of anything
you please. And therefore, Theætetus, knowledge cannot be
either perception, or true opinion, or the being able to give an
account also with true opinion. B

Theæt. It seems not.

Soc. Have we then any further ideas to be delivered of,
my friend, on this subject of knowledge, or have we now ·
given birth to all our conceptions?

Theæt. For myself, I protest, I have said (thanks to you)
even more than I had in me.

Soc. Then our obstetric art tells us that all these ideas
that have come forth from our brains are the offspring of empty
air, and not worth the bringing up.

Theæt. Assuredly so.

Soc. Well, Theætetus, if ever hereafter you should try to
breed other theories, or find yourself pregnant with some new
conception, you will be filled with better matter through our C
present investigations. Or if nothing should come of it, you
will at least give less trouble to your friends, and be more
gentle and tractable, for discreetly believing that you don't
know what you don't know. For thus far only does the power
of my art reach, and not beyond it: nor have I any knowledge
whatever on subjects which those are versed in who are or

have in past times become great and much looked up to for their learning. No! this midwife's practice my mother and I got by favour of the god; only she attends on women, while I am engaged with well-born youths, and such of my own sex as are good-looking. At present I must attend at the King's Portico to meet the accusation Meletus has brought against me.[1] In the morning, Theodore, let us meet here again.

D

[1] This little touch in the drama, which cannot be regarded in any way as historical, is introduced to show the imperturbable mind of Socrates, whom no anxiety, even on a matter immediately before him of life or death, could disengage from his philosophic speculations and his inquiry into truth.

THE END.

CAMBRIDGE: —PRINTED BY J PALMER

Breinigsville, PA USA
02 October 2009
225190BV00003B/3/P